KatyNation

Poe,
   Thanks for being a
great fen !
      Coach Mary Gaspel

Dexter Clay

Hello Poe — Thanks for
Your help to the *[illegible]*
      Coach Gayla Brown

Coach Poe
    Hope you enjoy this. You've
built traditionally strong programs
for years. Coach Mike Johnston

1

Also By Dexter Clay

Black Eye on America!

Walking with the Power

Only for a Season

Published by Black Eye World Publishing
Copyright 2007 by Black Eye World Publishing

Black Eye World Publishing
369 S. Doheny Dr.
Beverly Hills CA. 90211
Website:
www.katynation.com

ISBN 0-9665444-3-0
Printed and bound in the
United States by
Lighting Source

To the Universe

Thank you for teaching me that the power of our thoughts is real, and that through our positive thoughts, we can change the course of our lives and create a future that we can view with confidence.

Acknowledgments

As always, there are countless friends and family members who help support our efforts along the way that an author desires to thank when taking on a project like writing a book. In this book, I wish to single out a few special individuals whose love and support has allowed me to complete this project.

Gorman Morris

David Arnold

Robert Kramer
President, Westbound Bank, Katy, TX

Angela Thomason

Robert Willeby
Hands On Technical Support, Inc.

Lee Family
Gordon, Olinda, Kristyn, Amanda, Jordan, Jason, and Justyn Lee.

Michael Henderson

Clay family
Quincia, Carolyn, and Carl Clay.

Without question, this book is a testament to your belief in me.

Black Eye World Publishing
Special thanks
to the
Black Eye World Publishing Staff

Senior Editor   Rebecca Kemble

Co-Editors   Carolyn Wells,
                                 Quincia Clay,

Cover Design   Ramiro Reyna, Jr.

Photographer   Ramiro Reyna, Jr.

I thank you all for your commitment to this project.

KatyNation

The History of the Katy High School Football
Program
Table of Contents

KatyNation

The History of the Katy Football High School Program

When excellence becomes tradition, greatness has no limits.

22

District Championships

1948, 1958, 1959, 1961, 1962, 1963, 1964, 1986, 1989, 1992, 1994, 1995, 1996, 1997, 1998, 1999, 2000, 2001, 2003, 2004, 2005, 2006

"This place has a spirit to it that works through the program from the tiniest freshman to the head coach and into the community. It revolves around a positive history, and a passionate community who loves the boys. Probably 90% of the teams we play beat us on paper...that is height, weight, and ability. They'd kill us in a tug of war, They play with better talents; we try to and, fortunately, have, up to this point, played with better football players. It is a product of parents and a community who cares and understands the hearts of the coaching staff and trusts us with some of the best kids in the world.

"I've been tremendously blessed to work at Katy High School. I came in 2000, and the Tigers went 16-0 that year. I'm not sure I ever knew what was going on when we were at practice...it was a blur. I basically worked hard and tried not to get in the way. In 2003, we won State again. It was a totally different feeling. I felt like I had contributed to this one. I finally felt like a Katy Coach."

Gregg Miller
Defensive Coordinator/First Assist
2000 present

22

Bi-District Finalists

1948, 1958, 1959, 1963, 1964, 1986, 1988, 1989, 1991, 1992, 1994, 1995, 1996, 1997, 1998, 1999, 2001, 2002, 2003, 2004, 2005, 2006

"I left a defensive coordinator's job at a successful 5A high school to come to Katy High. I wanted to find out firsthand what many other coaches around Texas would like to know: 'How does Katy do it? Is it the community, the players, the coaches, the tradition?' It's all of those and much, much more!"

Coach Rich Slater
Defensive Line, 1st year

18

Area/Regional Finalists

1959, 1986, 1989, 1991, 1992, 1994, 1995, 1996, 1997, 1998, 1999, 2000, 2001, 2002, 2003, 2004, 2005, 2006

"It became very evident, very quickly, how much 'tradition' plays a part in the continued success of this team. When I arrived, the most significant thing I noticed was not the size, speed, or athletic ability of the players, but rather the number of kids in the program and the sincere intent on their part to maintain the winning tradition at Katy High School. It is a community effort in that it is important to so many people inside and outside of the program. The tradition is entrusted to each class, and there is an intense focus to not let the tradition of winning fade."

Coach Pat Dowling
Quarterback Coach
July of 2005 - Present

9

Regional Championships

1959, 1994, 1997, 1998, 1999, 2000, 2002, 2003, 2005

Athletic Trainer Motto: "No one cares how much you know until they know how much you care."

Taking care of Champions...

"Community Expectation, the willingness to be a team player and not just one of the eleven men on the field. Administrators, teachers and parents who allow coaches to coach, players to play, and parents to cheer and watch. The ability and trust between the team, that when we step out on the field, we believe we can win. This is how I explain what makes the Katy Tigers so great."

Justin "Doc" Landers
Head Athletic Trainer, 2002- Present

9

Regional Semi-Finalists

1992, 1998, 1999, 2000, 2002, 2003, 2004, 2005, 2006

"Any coach that wants to be around great coaches and kids strives to be at programs like Katy High School. It has been an awesome opportunity to be a part of this great tradition and contribute in some small way. Every day within this program is a chance to become a better person and coach. The winning tradition is wonderful, and many great coaches helped pave the way for the success that guys like me get to enjoy and now be a part of. I'm thankful every day for being here and having the opportunity to be a part of this place."

Coach Travis Ling
Strengthening/Conditioning Coordinator

11

Texas State Quarter Finalists

1959, 1992, 1994, 1997, 1998, 1999, 2000, 2002, 2003, 2004, 2005

"I graduated from Katy High School in 1997, and was a three year starter at inside linebacker and captain my senior year. I played college ball at Sam Houston State University, then got the opportunity to coach here in the fall of '02. This is my 5th year at Katy. My first two years, I coached the secondary, and now I coach inside linebackers, which is what I played. I have seen both parts of this program, as a player and now as a coach. Katy Football is the reason I got into coaching. I was pushed by my coaches...Bruno, Joseph, Johnston. They got more out of me that I thought I could give. They made me not only a better football player but also a better man. Now it is my turn to repay the favor, to give the future Tigers the same opportunities and experiences I had. Don't make excuses, and regrets last a lifetime."

Coach Todd Moebes
Inside Linebackers 2002-present

9

Texas State Semifinalists

1959, 1994, 1997, 1998, 1999, 2000, 2002, 2003, 2005

"The thing that stands out in my mind the most was the quote that I heard when I first got here. 'Those on the outside don't understand it. Those on the inside can't explain it.' This summed it all up for me."

Jeryl Brixey
Offensive Coordinator/Offensive Line Coach

8

Texas State Finalists

1959, 1994, 1997, 1998, 1999, 2000, 2003, 2005

"I have been around sports my entire life, and I have never seen anything that compares to Katy High School Football. The Katy Tiger 'Mystique' is bred in every athlete. If you asked me to define it, I wouldn't be able to, but if you ever come to watch the Tigers play - you would see it."

Debbie Decker
Assistant Director of Athletics-Administration

4

Texas State Championships

1959, 1997, 2000, 2003

The power of this program is found in the heartbeat of it's community.

Dexter Clay
Author of KatyNation

Foreword

I can honestly say that before there was *Friday Night Lights*, there was *KatyNation*. I am very thankful to H.G. Bissinger, author of *Friday Night Lights*, especially because he knew that there were countless stories in America about high school football. His wish was for other authors to follow him with works of their own. For his inspiration, I'm truly thankful.

When I give thanks for the inspiration of the book, I have to start with a complete stranger, a person to this day whose name I do not know. It was my first year in Los Angeles back in 1986. My first week there, I put in twelve applications for work. In less than two weeks, I had two jobs. One was as a model for Sak's Fifth Avenue in Beverly Hills and another was as a waiter at the Old World Restaurant on Beverly Drive. It was there that I went from a waiter to a host, to assistant manager, then to manager of the restaurant in less than two and a half weeks. I will always remember that time in my life, if for no other reason than I was living out of my truck at the time. It was in Beverly Hills that I learned that people perceive you by the way that you present yourself. No one has to know your situation but you.

Each morning around 5:00 a.m., I would first take Cricket, my Old English Sheepdog and trusted friend for a walk, and then I would drive over to UCLA and walk into a gym with my backpack over my shoulders. There, I would shower and shave and prepare myself for my two jobs. This went on for about a month and a half, until I could save enough for an overpriced L.A. apartment.

One quiet evening at the restaurant around about closing time, two very elegant and attractive women were sitting at a table, finishing a nice carrot cake which had helped to make the restaurant famous. As I made my rounds, one of the ladies smiled and asked to speak with me. I walked over, thinking that they wished to complain about something. They smiled and said, "We had a lovely evening tonight, but it seems as if we have left our wallets at home." I knew by the diamond rings which adorned three out of five fingers on their hands that they were only teasing me.

"Oh, that's okay," I said, "we have more than enough dishes for you two to wash back in the kitchen." We laughed, and they asked me to sit down.

They were the last two customers in the house, so I sat with them, and we shared laughs for a few minutes. Then one woman said something that I will always remember. She looked at me straight into my eyes and said, out of the clear blue, "I realize that you are here to be an actor, but your real rewards will come as a writer."

"Pardon me," I said, trying to assess where her statement came from.

"Yes, I see that you will be a writer someday."

"Are you sure that I'm not going to be a successful actor?" I replied, trying to come to my own defense.

"You will have a chance to act, but your real rewards will come as you write." I had already found that L.A. was filled with many "characters," so I just tucked that evening away as a delightful encounter.

KatyNation is my fourth book. The rewards that this attractive stranger spoke of have never been more apparent than in the passion I uncovered while writing this book. Walking into a community that I once thought to be something else, I found love for family, friends and community.

Entering the Katy community as a stranger, I came out as with something that has honestly changed my life. It was here that I found, lying underneath a successful football program, a writer's dream, the ability to become a part of my work. Here, I found a story that has the power to change people's lives, the power to equip them with something real and accessible to us all.

My real rewards will come as a writer, she said. To that stranger some twenty years ago I say, "Thank you. Today, I truly understand what you were preparing me for. My hope is that somehow I can manage to transfer what I have learned while writing this book to my readers." I want you to become aware of the basic elements that precede greatness and have a chance to embrace them all. May the rewards from reading this book open doors for you and follow you for days to come.

KatyNation
Prologue

It was the month of July 2005; I was driving back from Los Angeles, California for about the seventh time in my twenty-year stay there. My mother was having some health challenges, and I really did not know what to expect when I arrived home. For those who have never been to Los Angeles, it is a city like none other in the world. So many different nationalities are trying to find the secret to help them get ahead of the game of life. With that desire, they bring with them all the positives and negatives of humanity.

For me, this drive back was much different than the rest. A part of me felt as if it might be my last trip. To me, this meant turning away from many unfulfilled dreams of my own. Ironically, I was leaving the city for the same reasons that I left Texas twenty years earlier. It was that old empty feeling that a person gets when he feels like he simply doesn't belong. I just knew in my heart that it was time to move on.

You never know what the day might bring you. It is much like being on a roller coaster. Once that baby climbs to its highest point, whether you like it or not, you had better hang on for the ride. No matter how nauseating or exciting you think that ride might be, there is one thing that's for sure, at some point you understand that it's time to get off.

I had just come up to the border of El Paso Texas. I didn't have to see any signs that said, "Welcome to El Paso;" all I had to do was turn on the radio. Yep, all you get is country, country, and more country music on the airwaves. Whoever said that Nashville was the country music capital has obviously never driven through El Paso before. It was like driving into a wall of country music, but being a Texas native, that was okay with me.

I still had another eight hours of driving before I reached my destination of Houston. One of the great things about driving from California to Texas is the healing time that you encounter as you move on down the road. The time to reflect on one's life is something that should never be taking for granted. To me, the greatest benefit of driving alone is the opportunity to hear yourself think while cruising the open highway. In my mind, this has to be one of the greatest forms of therapy available.

My inner voice kept reminding me of how close I came to making big things happen in Los Angeles. However, even though I had a great stay, each mile that brought me closer to Houston presented me with the reality that, again, I had fallen short of my ultimate dreams.

"San Antonio 35 Miles," the sign said!

"Well I'm all most home. I can't believe that I'm going to be living in Texas again. This has got to be a bad dream," I thought to myself, again. This time, I heard myself saying it out loud. Even though it was pitch black dark on the open highway, I still felt like a cloud was hanging over my head. I had been told that Texas had changed considerably over the last twenty years. I had only mediocre memories of my time in Texas which forced me twenty years earlier to realize that I needed to see more of life, and leaving Texas would be a good start.

A few miles outside a small Texas town called Katy, tears begin to fall from my face. I had almost arrived home, and I wasn't sure what home would offer me. I'm not really sure why I felt I had to dump all my pent-up emotions on this little city located a few miles west of Houston.

Even through my emotions, I could see that Katy had changed somewhat. It used to be this little two-lane highway.

Now, it was difficult to see where Houston began and Katy ended. Through the flood of emotions, I felt a smile begin to force its way through my face. You see Katy Texas, was now the home of my best friend in the whole world, a guy with whom I had played football at Eisenhower High School.

I didn't know it at the time, but it would be in this small town just a little outside of Houston, where I would stumble across a story that needed to be told. It would be in this open range filled with Wal*Marts, Home Depots, and thousand of yards of fresh new highway that I would find something very special, something that would create a wonderful change in my life.

If there is such a thing as finding a needle in a haystack, this is the opportunity that was about to be presented me. A chance to stumble across an incredible story. A writer's dream-come-true.

It was a few months after I had returned to Houston before I was made aware of my true purpose for returning. My friend called me up one day and asked, "Hey what are you doing tonight?"

"I have no real plans," I replied.

"Well why don't you come in for dinner, and then we can go see Katy play CyFalls in a playoff game." I had never been to a Katy football game, so I thought that it would be a good way to pass the evening. As we drove over to Tulley Stadium, my buddy had a little smirk on his face.

"Hey man, what are you grinning like a cat for?"

"Dex, you are not going to believe what you are about to see."

"What do you mean?"

"Well it's hard to describe. You just have to see it for yourself."

"See what?"

" Just be patient," he said, "we are almost there." By that time, we were just pulling off of Interstate 10. I noticed the traffic jam being created ahead of us.

"Man, this is almost as bad as the L.A. traffic," I said. He just kept smiling. As I looked closer at the cars, I began to see that the automobiles were all painted with red and white or logos of Katy Tigers. There were signs on the SUV's saying, "Go Tigers"

"Hey, don't tell me that all these people are headed for the game!" The grin on my friend's face just got bigger. About thirty minutes later, we finally found a place to park. Even in the parking lot, which was about two blocks away from the stadium, the atmosphere was buzzing with energy.

My buddy and I walked up from the west end of the stadium. It was then I knew what he had been grinning about all this time. It was the first time that I had seen the KatyNation. Hundreds and thousands of Katy fans gathered in one place to cheer on their local team.

All I could think of to say was, "Oh, my God! This is unbelievable! This is a *high school* football game?" Before me, lay a sea of red and white, blanketing the entire half of the stadium. "This is something out of a movie!" I said out loud. I knew right then and there, without a shadow of a doubt, why my life had brought me back to Texas.

I didn't have to question why this place and time had been given to me. I was a writer who had been devoid of something special to share with the world. In front of me was the physical manifestation of a book. Though it had not been written, I saw it in countless unknown faces swirling in front of me.

Maybe it was the fact that by living in Los Angeles I learned to see things a little differently than most of the world. While most would see simply the excitement of a high

24

school football game, I saw the opening to a remarkable story. I knew why I had been invited to see the Tigers play that evening. At that moment in time, I knew my purpose; there was no question to why I found myself living in Texas again. It was as if a small window from the universe opened up briefly to me and said, "Here take this; it is yours." I hope that you will enjoy *KatyNation (The History of Katy High School Football).*

Birth of a Nation

To appreciate the evolved state of Katy, Texas, today, one should go back to its beginning, its conception, if you may. The first real records of Katy fall around 1843. However, before I discuss Katy, Texas, I would like to take a moment to acknowledge the Native Americans who are so often forgotten as writers recreate their stories about American life. Frequently, the passage of time makes it easy for writers to do that, to put aside those who came before us. Maybe it is simply human nature to forget about aspects of our past that we find difficult to digest. I believe that when we do this, we somehow cheat ourselves of the rightful power of our heritage.

I have a theory that if we learn to acknowledge those who came before us in truth, honesty and thanksgiving, we somehow gain a better understanding of our present and future. Today's KatyNation was once roamed by race of Native Americans known as the Coco Indians.

According to *The Online Handbook of Texas*, the Coco Indians were part of the nomadic "Karankawans who lived near the Gulf Coast, between the Lavaca and Brazos rivers." Reportedly, they also hunted in the area we now call Katy. "They were most frequently linked with the lower Colorado River in the area now covered by Colorado, Wharton, and Matagorda counties..... In the latter half of the Eighteenth

Century, the Coco were represented at various Spanish missions.... Some of the Coco remained in their ancestral area along the lower Colorado River, where Anglo-American colonists encountered them in the early Nineteenth Century. Later, these Coco merged with remnants of other Karankawan groups and also became known as Karankawas. The Karankawa Indians became extinct by 1858."

Quite often, while researching American history we stumble across episodes that seem cold and inhuman. To say that any race of human beings have become extinct makes my spirit uneasy.

Though the Karankawa are said to be extinct, I believe that only the physical body or being can become extinct, that the spirit of a culture or community continues to manifest itself throughout time. Here's a question to grumble over, what if there is a possibility that the spirit of the early Karankawa Indians is still found in Katy Texas? It could be "just me," but if you have ever strolled around an empty Jack Rhodes Stadium, you may have noticed that there is something slightly mystical about the open fields which surround the stadium to the east. Especially when a light breeze rushes up to catch your face and dances on past you into the treetops.

The first record of inhabitants of Cane Island was in the year 1894. By the way, Cane Island Creek is what we know as Katy, Texas today. In "A History of Katy, Texas," from KatyTexas.com, Susan DeVries Barwis reports that the first family is said to have settled on Christmas Day in 1894. Barwis adds, "Mr. William Pitts, his wife Lella, and their three children came from the town of Pattison, Texas. [Shortly after,] in 1895, many more families came to find new farms and new lives. The Peeks came from Indiana and Iowa to farm and run dairies. The Stuarts and the Danovers came from Iowa. The Beckendorffs came from Pattison to farm. Mr. Cabiness came then, too. He worked for the railroad as the depot agent. He also built a lumberyard, milled rice, bought and sold the farmers' peanuts, and helped start the Apostolic Faith Church in 1905."

Now I know to many of you, these names and dates mean nothing. However, in order to understand our heritage, we must be aware of its beginnings. These names at one time had faces that bring us closer to our own images. According to Barwis, one such face was that of Mr. James Oliver Thomas, who came from Mississippi. He bought 320 acres of land and laid out the town site of Katy in 1895. Mr. Thomas set aside land for two parks. One park was located on Cane Island Creek, and the other was the town square.

"In 1896, the migration to the Katy area continued with the Stockdick family, the Ruskeys, the Mortons, and David Peter Franz, a watchmaker." Hmmm, the Mortons, could they be the ancestors of those whom the new $68,000,000 high school in Katy ISD is named after? If I am not mistaken, doesn't that school find itself nestled off of Franz Road? See how history has a way of giving us a better understanding of the present?

Coming from Iowa, Mr. Stockdick didn't work for Century 21 or ReMax, but he was a real estate person and is said to have encouraged many other families to move from the northern areas to Katy, Texas, according to *Katy Magazine Online.* Barwis from KatyTexas.com, adds, "1896 was also the year Katy was first listed in Washington, D.C. as having a post office.... Mr. J.O. Thomas was the postmaster." In some ways, you can say that Katy, Texas, was officially born into the world that year.

"The next year, 1897, saw the arrival of the Morrisons from Missouri, the Freemans from Iowa, and the Eule family from Germany," Barwis continues. She adds that the Eules were said to be the first rice farmers in Katy. Instead of buying a box of Uncle Ben's rice, how does Uncle Eule's Rice sound to you? Oh well, what's in a name? More importantly, Barwis says that the Eule family had a school in their home for their own children and the children of their neighbors. (And you thought that home schooling was some kind of new concept!) Well, the fact is that home schooling was the origin of most school districts of today.

Here's a trivia question for all you Baptist folk out there. Who was the first to pastor the first Baptist church in Katy? Okay, time is up! Barwis says that it was Mr. Featherston; the year was 1898. In addition, she says that the first doctor arrived in Katy in 1898 in the form of Dr. James Malcolm Stewart. He came from Tennessee with his new wife to start his medical practice.

Another Katy first came in the form of John Henry Wright, his brother Wilbur, and their parents. Barwis reports, "They drove their team of horses and wagons from Missouri.... The families stayed to farm and later started a drug store. In 1904, Mr. J. H Wright and Dr. Stewart formed a partnership. Mr. Wright opened a drugstore with Dr. Stewart's office next door.

"Two more families arrived on the same train in 1900. Both families had moved from Germany to Iowa to farm, and then, the Schlipfs and the Weinmans made Katy their home. They purchased farms north of town, and there they started their new lives. The Eule farm was nearby, so the children went to school in the Eule's home. Soon the classes were moved to the Schlipf home, and then, they were moved to the schoolhouse that was built on the Schlipf's land. Children attended the country school until it closed in 1918. All children living on the farms went to school at home or at a neighbor's house.

"In 1918, all the children from the small farm schools were brought together in the town of Katy to start the Katy Independent School District. Children came from Cobb School, Schlipf School, Dishman School and Sills School."

Cane Island Creek became Katy, Texas, which has six high schools, a career and technology school, and an alternative campus. Katy ISD is one of the fastest-growing school districts in the Houston metropolitan area, as well as in the state. Katy boasts a student population of over 44,646.

Today's projections show a steady upswing throughout this decade, with total enrollment topping 70,000 students by 2013. I think that it is safe to say that Katy ISD has come a long way from its humble beginning of 263 students back in 1934, a school district that got its beginning in 1918 made up of the farms of Schlipf and Sills and brought together with the help of Mr. C. I Baird.

They were a community of families much like we see today in Katy. Sure, times have changed. However, the fact that has become increasingly clear to me is the undeniable presence of a kindred spirit that lies within the community of Katy, Texas.

For those of us who have had the opportunity to walk through this very special town just a few miles west of Houston, there is unequivocally a great peace that permeates the area. A powerful sense of community and passion for life has settled here from many years before. Very special people who have given us a great foundation on which to build have also left us something remarkable.

My first stop into town was at the old railroad depot. It sits right in the heart of Old Katy. You can recognize it by the bright red caboose, which stands alone a few yards to the east of it. I thought that by stopping by here, I would find some knowledge which would help me to be better acquainted with the history of Katy. Near the ramp leading to the doorway of the building, there was an historical marker to the right which gave a brief synopsis of the life of the MKT, Missouri Kansas Texas Railroad.

Inside, I met this very charming woman about seventy years of age. Her name was Betty Calwell. She was very polite and was helping to give directions to another lady already there before me. After the lady walked out, I introduced myself and explained to Betty that I was writing a book about Katy High School football and that I was doing research on the history of the city of Katy.

As I look back on my time there, I can't help but feel that Betty really and truly enjoyed working in the old train station. She gave a brief tour of the once-two-room building, to which, in the early 1900s, another room had been added. To view the interior of the old building was like stepping back into time. The original wooden floors were still in very good condition. Betty even commented that things were built better "way back when," because people actually built things with the concept that they should last. I had to agree with her. She continued to present me with little interesting bits of data and information from the Heritage Society of Katy.

A wonderful aspect of many senior people of age is that they really enjoy taking the time and patience to share history with you. The younger generation seems to be so rushed to "get there fast." Maybe it is because the older people feel like a part of the history that they like to share.

I felt in a way that the old train station was Betty's home. She seemed to be so knowledgeable about every artifact in the place. I will never forget one point in our conversation. We heard the whistle of an in-coming train. Betty got up and said, "Excuse me, I have to wave at the engineer." I got up to follow her to the door, and she stepped outside to the small landing. As the big engine slowly passed by, Betty smiled and waved as if she were a young schoolgirl. I asked her, "Betty do you know the engineer?"

"No," she replied. "I just always come out to wave."

I think by the big smile on the engineer's face and the sound of his horn that maybe there was a little old-fashioned flirting going on. I smiled as we both went back inside. Betty continued to present me with information about Katy. At one point, she shared with me that she still had season tickets to the Katy Tiger football games. She even shared a brief story of one of the first championship games for Katy High School. She said that the whole town was so excited that everyone in town left to go to the game except for one man and one woman. Betty told me that the entire town of Katy was completely abandoned. She said that the fire departments of the neighboring cities kept an eye on the town while every man, woman and child went to cheer for their local team. I was smiling from ear to ear.

I knew that this was the kind of story that would make *KatyNation* come to life.

Each person whom I encountered seemed to solidify my realization that I had stumbled across a story which simply had to be shared. As I completed my hour of Betty's time, she told me that I should spend some time with Katy's mayor. She said that he embodied the spirit of the town of Katy and to make sure that I met him. I told her that I would. I stood up and walked over to shake Betty's hand.

I felt as if the special gift that I had been given unwrapped itself every time I met someone who had knowledge about the Katy Tiger football program. Every person gave me the opportunity to see something different about the Katy community. This was the beginning of what was in store for me; this journey would be a special one, the most rewarding time in my entire life. Walking back to my truck, I kept telling myself that there was something mystical about this town, that I had not even begun to scratch the surface, and that as I continued my research for this book, I just knew that my life would be changed forever.

No. 1 Fan
Elnora Hudgens

I originally heard of the Number One Katy fan at the 2006 Red-White spring game. This was my first "up close and personal" view of the Katy football team. Pacing the sidelines, I was amazed at the excitement that was permeating Jack Rhodes Stadium. There was so much pre-game activity going on that it was almost intoxicating. The team was going through its stretching and warm up routines. Coaches were directing their drills as if they were the proud parents of each kid on the field. Cheerleaders were bouncing up and down on the turf like they had jumping beans in their shoes.

What astonished me was the number of fans in the stadium that evening. The home side was completely packed. There were even a few stragglers hanging out on the visitor side of the stadium. The home side reflected a sea of red and white, as if it were a district playoff game.

The pre-game activities included the recognition of a group of special Olympic athletes known as the Katy Wolf Pack. As each member was introduced, a Katy football team member escorted him up the sideline. Looking into the eyes of these young people as they marched past me, it was apparent that they understood that there was something very special about being a part of the Katy football community.

All that was happening around me energized me. I stopped one of the passing coaches. "This is simply amazing."

His name was Coach Landers, and his reply was direct and to the point, "Yes it is!" Shaking his head up and down, "Yes it is," he said again as his eyes sparkled, looking up in the direction of the Katy community.

I took that moment to introduce myself. He said that he had heard about me because I was writing a book about the history of the program. Then Coach Landers said something that I will always remember. He said, "This is a special community. But there is a lady that is considered Katy's Number One fan. She is probably up in those stands right now. Her name is Elnora Hudgens, and she has been coming to Katy football games since 1959. As a matter of fact," he said, "she lives right down the street from the stadium."

Writing this information, I thought that meeting her might help to give me some insight to what was so special about the Katy football community. I knew if I could speak with someone who had a long-standing appreciation for this program, that somehow this would at least put me in the right direction needed to carry on this project.

By halftime, Rhodes Stadium was a mini-Super Bowl of excitement. It seems that a new tradition of auctioning off a signed football and helmet had found its way into the program. Coach Joseph introduced the auctioneer to the fans. All of the proceeds of the items went to the Katy Booster Club. This was an organization that I planned to research thoroughly because it was responsible for contributing thousands of dollars to the athletic program each year.

One must never underestimate the power of mothers and fathers who truly wish to support their children's schools. Maybe I should not have been surprised that the autographed helmet went for $3,500. However, what I was impressed with was that the owners of the Hanson Construction Company purchased the souvenir, then turned around and donated it back to the Booster Club, so that it could auction off the same helmet again. In all, the Booster Club raised over eight thousand dollars that evening.

Walking back to my car that evening after the game, I could not help but think that this Katy football community seemed to manifest itself in several ways, that its success was a combination of many different efforts. There was definitely something very powerful in this community, and I felt each step led me towards a better understanding of it.

It was a couple of days after the Red-White game that I started my search for Katy's Number One Fan. I knew in my heart that Katy was comprised of thousands of Number One Fans. However, for some reason I knew that Coach Landers was trying to tell me something important when he pointed me into the direction of Elnora Hudgens. Whatever he was trying to tell me, I was going to find out.

Even though I did not have an address to Miss Hudgens' house, I did remember that Coach Landers had mentioned that she was living somewhere across the street from the church on 11th Street. It was Friday morning around ten o'clock when I found myself driving past the church. Unsure of just what I might find, I noticed a gentlemen apparently in his late seventies walking around in his front yard. So I pulled my truck over and got out. Walking up to him I smiled. "Good morning sir, my name is Dexter Clay, and I am writing a book called *KatyNation* about the history of Katy High School football."

Before I could say another word, he smiled back and said, "Well, young man, you have come to the right place. The lady next door is a huge Katy fan. My name is Barry," he said, holding out his hand. "You have surely come to the right place. Elnora has been following Katy football since she was in school there. She's not home right now; she's probably at the hospital. Her mother has been very ill, but I'm sure she would not mind if I gave you her telephone number. Come on inside, and I will get it for you."

Waiting for me as I went to get my keys out of the truck, Barry walked in front of me into the garage and opened the door leading into his home. He shared with me that he had lived there several years and that he had lost his wife a few years back. His home was very warm, and everything seemed to be in order. I really did not think about it then, but this gentleman didn't seemed to be bothered with the fact that I was a complete stranger. His mild and gentle spirit seemed to be at peace with everything around him. Picking up the Caller ID connected to his phone, he called out the numbers while I wrote them down.

Back outside, Barry shared a few thoughts about various topics. He warned me that Elnora truly liked to talk and suggested that I bring lots of pens and paper. Then he stopped to look underneath his car parked in the driveway. "What are you looking for?" I asked.

"Oh, that dang head cover on the weed eater went flying off, and I can't find it anywhere."

"Well, I will help you look for it," I said as he continued to search around the car. I started to search completely across the other side of the yard. Sure enough, there it was. "Here it is, Sir!"

"Well, I was standing way over here when that thing shot off. I never would have thought that it would have run way over there. Thank you, young man."

"No, it is I who should thank you, Sir. I do appreciate you taking the time to get me Elnora's telephone number."

I honked my horn as I drove off from Barry's home. I wondered what he meant when he said that Elnora had a rasp in her voice. It was early evening when I contacted Miss Hudgens for the first time. She was not in, so I simply left her a message, introducing myself. It was the first of many messages that I would leave to people living in the Katy community about this project.

A few days later, I got this call from an older lady. I really had to concentrate to hear her voice over the phone. Filled with excitement, Elnora apologized for taking so long to get back with me. She explained that her mother had experienced some very trying times at the hospital during the last few weeks. I told her that I completely understood and thanked her for taking the time to get back with me. We spoke over the phone for about twenty minutes. One thing that Elnora was not hurting from was the ability to create conversation.

At the end of the conversation, I asked her if after her mother got better we could get together. She suggested that I come up to the hospital one afternoon. I told her that I did not want to intrude, but she assured me that it would help her to break up the routine of her day. I eventually agreed, and we set up Thursday afternoon at 2:30 for our interview. Wow! I could not believe that she was so excited to talk to me about the book!

Later, I found out why she was so excited. Elnora, for some reason, thought I was Clyde Drexler, the famous ex-Houston Cougar and Houston Rocket basketball player. Dexter Clay, Clyde Drexler. I could see how Elnora could have made the association. That comparison was okay until she said that Clyde had a better jump shot than me. Well, that really hurt. Okay, so just maybe it was the truth, but I would never admit it.

Pulling up into the parking lot of Herman Memorial Hospital in Katy, I was not really sure what to expect. I never really liked hospitals much. Maybe it was the distinctive odor that seemed to accompany that environment that helped me to feel uneasy about hospitals. However, this was where this story had taken me, and any good writer will tell you that he goes where the story takes him.

Walking into the lobby, I was greeted by three elderly ladies, all seated behind a large counter area. I signed in and asked them the direction for Room 206. "Take the elevator to the second floor, then take a left."

"Thank you," I said, and found myself standing in the elevator waiting for the door to open.

When I stepped onto the second floor, I was greeted by that odor that I found so familiar about hospitals. I'm not sure if it is the chemicals used to clean and disinfect them or the different medications distributed throughout the hospitals. I approached another reception area and was directed down the hall to Room 206.

After the meeting, I could not sleep, and it was about 3:00 in the morning when I pulled the small tape recording out of my briefcase. I'm not sure why I chose this time of day to gather all my thoughts and begin placing them on paper. If I had to take a guess, it would have to be the fact that most of the world was asleep, allowing the universe an opportunity to slow down a bit. Maybe at this time all the demands placed on the world had been given a chance to relax, making it easier for me to think.

One thing that I know for sure is that my mind seemed fresher and more than willing to perform at this hour of the morning. I kept going back to the moment when I walked into hospital Room 206. My thoughts were as vivid as if I had just walked into the room. My eyes caught the smile of a lady, fragile, yet strong-minded, sitting next to a patient lying in a bed. "Excuse me," I said.

"Oh hi, you must be Drexler," the lady said with a very raspy voice.

"I'm Dexter Clay," I replied. She slowly got up from her chair to shake my hand.

I set the tape recorder on my desk, got out my notepad, and reflected about meeting Elnora Hudgens, one of Katy's Number One Fans. I strongly remember her introducing me to her mother. I could tell her mother was fighting a battle for life. Elnora spoke in her right ear, reminding her that I was the writer that she told her about. Her mother had just been given a feeding tube that morning. I could see that it left her very uncomfortable. She kept trying to raise her fragile arms to pull at the tube that was lodged in her right nostril.

I tried not to show it, but for that moment, I was very angry with God. I wanted to question Him, "Why this ninety-three year old person have to be in that condition?" There was no doubt that I lost sight of why I was there while I asked Elnora question after question about her mother's condition.

I'm sure the lady in the bed next to her mother must have thought I was some kind of a doctor. Elnora told her mother that she was going down the hall to the waiting room and asked if she needed anything. With just a small head gesture and her eyes, she relayed the response, "No." Elnora pulled her little aluminum walker towards her and started to make her way to the door into the hall of the hospital.

Sitting down at my desk, I reached for the recorder, clicking the rewind button. I could hear the tape spin back towards the front of the tape. About ten seconds later, a loud click halted its progression. Placing the button on "Play," I adjusted the volume at the same time. It was this moment that I realized that *KatyNation* was not about writing a book. It was about becoming a part of people's lives. It was at that moment that I knew I must ask for both guidance and direction in order to document this history with which I somehow found myself becoming entwined.

Watching the two small wheels begin to turn forward in the window of the recorder, I returned to that afternoon with a person who would help me better understand the history of Katy High School football.

"Elnora, I hope that you don't mind if I record this. Also, I will be writing as we go along. It just helps to be able to go back to your actual words later on."

"Please feel free!" she said.

"How long have you lived in Katy, Elnora?"

"I was born in Baytown in 1944. My parents moved to Katy when I was one, and I have been here ever since. You know, I was not expected to live when I was born. When I was ten and a half months, I contracted meningitis, which left me unconscious for five days and five nights. I carried a fever of 105 degrees. They could only feed me goat's milk. This is the reason why today my voice is the way it sounds."

I reflected on what the times might have been like back then. In many ways, medicine has made great strides. Elnora stopped a passing nurse as she made her rounds, snapping my thoughts back to reality. She was asking the nurse questions her about her mother's doctor for the evening rounds. Then she got back to her story.

"Did I tell you that my father was the mayor of Katy at one time?"

"No, you didn't not mention that yet," I replied.

"His name was John Eugene Hudgens. My dad was a city councilman and mayor, and as mayor, he never lost a race. He was honest, a good Christian," she said, "and he always treated everyone fairly."

I asked her in what years he had served, but she did

not recall. She did recall that there were a little over one thousand people living in Katy about that the time of the big 1959 game.

Looking over to see the recorder still rolling, I could tell that Katy's Number One Fan was going to be a wealth of knowledge for me. She described how empty the city was at the time of the '59 championship game. "Most people got up around 4:00 a. m. to start their journey. By 6:30 a.m., the entire city of Katy was empty. In fact, there were only about ten people left in town for that game. We used to make a joke that whoever was the last person to leave Katy should turn out the lights. In fact," she said, "we had to get the neighboring cities' police and fire departments to watch our little city. It was like a ghost town."

"I bet you never met a woman who knows as much about football as I do, have you?" I smiled and continued to jot notes in my journal. "You know, I am still a member of the Katy Alumni Board of Directors. That's right, I am the Chairman of PR. In fact, we are getting ready to have our forty-five year reunion coming up this June." You might want to try to make that."

"Well, if I am in town, I will just try to do my best," I said.

"While you are in Katy, you need to stop by the Brookshire Brothers pharmacy if you can and ask for a man by the name of James Watson. James is a friend of mine, and I think that he was in the band back then. James has in his pharmacy a picture of the boys that played on the 1959 championship team."

Even though I was recording this, I was writing down all this information as fast I could. I didn't really know where this information was going to lead me. I knew that as long as I followed the leads, this story would write itself. This was my plan of attack: I was simply going to write this book as it was presented to me. Sometimes as a writer you just have to trust that your research has the ability to direct and determine its own course.

"James used to play in the band back in 1959. He would be a really good person to talk to. He still sees a lot of the people that lived around Katy back in that time. I always felt that he was a pretty good friend of mine back in school."

Elnora took the time to stop another nurse as she passed in the hallway. She was sharing her thoughts with me about Katy football, but it was easy to see that she had the ability to address the real issues when it came to her mother's health. My interview with her went on for about an hour and fifteen minutes. One of the points that seemed to register with me was that I could see how passionate she was about the community of Katy. This was the aspect that I wanted to emphasize.

I didn't have to ask Elnora a lot of questions. Once I turned on the recorder, she just sort of put the conversation on automatic pilot and never stopped talking. Eventually she covered the ground that I wanted to discuss. All I had to do was just keep writing and letting the recorder do its job.

It was a little after 5:00 a.m., when I looked at the clock. I didn't realize that I had been transferring the recording to paper for that long, stopping the tape and rewinding it over and over to make certain that I could pick up Elnora's every word.

When I compiled my newly-acquired information, it seemed that my biggest leads were found in James Watson and Douglas Gilbert. Thus, the next day I was off to Katy again. This time I was stopping by the Brookshire Brothers pharmacy.

It was a pleasant drive in 4:00 p.m. traffic when I

arrived in Katy. I didn't have to deal with the 610 Loop and the congestion of the Beltway 8 cars. I had figured out that, if I took West Little York to Eldridge, I could literally bypass the major traffic spots. Hey, my few months as a limo driver back in L.A. at least carried some perks. The fastest way from Point A to Point B is not always a straight line, especially when it is a line filled with Houston's commuters.

Pulling into the parking lot of Brookshire Brothers, I smiled when I looked up to see a sign that said, "Since 1921." I felt like I was stepping back in time to recover some priceless information. I was on a kind of treasure hunt, and the entire city of Katy was my treasure map. Walking in, I could see that the pharmacy was over to the far left corner of the store. I found myself slowly walking over to that particular area, not quite sure just what to expect, but eagerly awaiting whatever I would find. Closer to the courtesy counter, a huge portrait caught my eye. It was a picture of the players of the 1959 Katy High School football team.

There it stood, overlooking everything, as if it were standing guard over the store. I stood for what had to be two or three minutes. "Sir, sir, can I help you?" I looked to see one of the attendants trying to get my attention. "Oh hi," I said. "How old is that picture?"

"I'm not sure, but Mr. Watson can tell you; he's the oldest one here," she replied, with this huge grin on her face. A few seconds later, a very kind-hearted looking man came out from the back area.

After I introduced myself, I shared with him my reason for being so intrigued with the old photograph. He then began to share the history of the team with me. "If you are writing a book, then you will need to talk with a gentlemen by the name of Charlie Shafer. You can reach him right here in Katy; he works for the tax assessor's office I believe." I could tell that those must have been great times in Mr. Watson's life. He smiled as he shared the information about the old picture.

At least until his boss walked up. Actually, it was his wife. James was the personable one. You could tell that Mrs. Watson was the one who kept things moving around there. She, too, was very pleasant, yet she conveyed a firmness that seemed to deliver the message of who was really in charge of the pharmacy. Apparently, they were high school sweethearts, and it was easy to see that they had a very special bond between them. She took a second and wrote down Charlie Shafer's name for me.

"Thank you so much for your time. I would like to come back and chat with you and James again at another time, if that is okay." She smiled and said that would be fine.

Exiting the store, I took a moment to stop by the deli to grab a sandwich. I sat down to devour it before moving on. As I sipped a little soda out of the straw in my cup, something caught my eye. On the walls of the seating area of the deli, someone had placed pictures of the old Katy community. I got up to take a closer look at the photographs. Each one took me further and further back in time. There was a mystique about these old pictures which beckoned me to look beyond what I saw and somehow recognize how far we had come from that time period.

In each picture, I saw the city of Katy in its infancy of sorts. I could see in the eyes of the strangers who were present before me that each individual was a priceless part of the young town known as Katy. In a way, they were saying that they were creating something that would be very special someday. Whoever wrote that a picture was worth a thousand words really knew the power of that statement.

Leaving the deli section of Brookshire Brothers

grocery store, I wondered if the everyday customer realizes the power of the small shrine of pictures that adorns the walls, physical evidence of a past that gives us a silent look into the future of the community that we call Katy.

No. # 46 Charlie Shafer
Just for the Record

That evening, I called Information for the phone number of the Municipal Offices of Katy, Texas. "Yes, thank you Operator, I need the office of a Mr. Charlie Shafer please." I'm was not very sure why Mr. Watson had pointed out the young face of # 46 in the picture. I knew, however, as this story continued to unfold, that I would eventually find out. It was early Tuesday morning when I scheduled my meeting with Charlie. I likened pulling up outside the municipal office of Katy to being beamed back into a time warp. The town of Katy still carries that vintage rustic energy that says change is not always the best thing.

The quiet city streets with more than ample parking were a nice change of pace from the hustle and bustle of big city life. The presence of the old buildings helped to make the visit into town seem a little more inviting. I smiled when I pulled up to an empty parking space. It was hard to think that there were parking spaces in this country that didn't have parking meters connected to them. One of the things you quickly learned about big city life was that every available parking space had a parking meter growing out of it. In fact, in areas of Los Angeles, it would cost you a quarter for every seven minutes of parking time. It was easy to see how the (DOT) Department Of Transportation was a $91-million-a-year institution.

I soon found myself standing inside the quiet building where Charlie worked. A very charming lady greeted me. I told her that I had a 10:00 a.m. appointment with Mr. Shafer. She simply yelled over her left shoulder, " Charlie your 10:00 is here. Go on in, dear!" When I met Charlie, I kept visualizing him in his uniform. Charlie was one of the lucky ones to whom time had been generous. His small frame and gray hair gave no signs that he had been a "super jock" in his past. Dressed in a pair of jeans and a burgundy shirt, Charlie seemed to be as gentle as a lamb. Of course, I don't think that the deer head that hung up on his back wall would have agreed.

While I told him what I was trying to accomplish with the book, I could see his energy begin to move into excitement. I was not sure of Charlie's role with the Tiger squad of 1959, but I was about to find out.

The conversation went on for about forty-five minutes. I could not help but enjoy the role of being a writer. The excitement of researching and of meeting people, coming into their world as a stranger, and hopefully leaving as a friend was great to me.

Charlie told me that there were only about fifty-three kids in his senior class in 1960. He mentioned to me that I should try to contact the old Head Coach of the Tigers Gordon Brown. I will not forget the look on his face as he suggested that I locate his former coach.

I'm not sure that coaches truly understand the power that they carry in a kid's life. When Charlie spoke of Coach Brown, I could see the pride in Charlie's face while he spoke of someone much like a father. "Also, if you truly want to find out about early Katy football, then you should contact my father-in-law Melvin Jordan." He said that Melvin played on one of the six man teams.

He said that the older man's team might have even worn leather helmets back then. The mention of the old leather helmets really made me feel like I was beginning to uncover an authentic part of Katy football history, a history that I was hoping would somehow give me a better understanding of the somewhat mystical energy that the community of Katy possesses in the spirit of its football program. Well, at least in my mind, anyway.

Charlie shared with me the names of some of the players on the 1959 squad. I remember him mentioning that their fullback, a kid by the name of Farriel Culpepper, #47, was the stud on the team. It seemed that Katy ran what was considered the veer play back then, and Culpepper was the workhorse who made it happen for the Katy Tigers.

Charlie was such an humble and quiet man; it took all that I had to get him to admit that it was he who was responsible for the game-winning touchdown that gave the Tigers the 1959 State Championship.

I think that I was more excited about the fact I had stumbled across this than he was. I felt time continuing to write its story about us all…that the kids who play the game of football all across this country don't quite understand the full importance of the pictures that time takes of them. While living in the present, we rarely realize that time is recording our every effort until the past is unfolded.

My meeting with Charlie Shafer was special. It was my first real contact with someone who was actually present on the field in 1959. Leaving his office, I was overcome by the feeling of being blessed by the opportunity to write this story. I knew that I would eventually uncover the great mystery behind an outstanding football program.

Doug Gilbert #74
1959 Team

The following day, I received a phone call from a gentleman by the name of Doug Gilbert. It appeared that Elnora was kind enough to pass along my name and number to him. It appeared that this whole project was taking on a life of its own. My only hope was to get out of the way and let *KatyNation* run its own course. I have learned that most things happen better if you give them room to breathe. They just seem to manifest themselves and mature naturally.

Doug and I agreed that we would meet early Saturday afternoon. It just so happened that he was going to be in Katy that day. He called me as he was leaving his home in Cypress around about 11:30 a.m. that morning. I was already in a Katy park under a huge oak tree whose great limbs covered half of the street. It was a perfect spot to wait for Doug. Gathering my thoughts, trying to analyze the questions that I wanted to ask him, I felt extremely excited about the possibilities of what I might learn from this perfect stranger who was kind enough to include me into his world and not think anything of it.

11:54 a.m. My phone rang, and it was Doug. "I am just a few minutes outside Katy, where are you?" he asked.

"I'm parked on 6th Street and Katyland Drive," I said.

"Oh, good! Why don't we meet at McDonald's restaurant on Highway 90? Do you know where it is?"

I said I would meet him there in a few minutes.
Arriving a few minutes before Doug, I found a table. It is a funny thing about the inside of a McDonald's restaurant. No

matter how many of them that we frequent over the years, they always seem to be the same on the inside, built to serve the masses in the most efficient way possible. If in fact McDonald's were the measuring stick of America's need to deliver (and right away), it would become obvious that we have become a nation of impatient people. Even with a full house, the average customer can be served in less than 120 seconds after arriving. You can have your food and be finished eating in less than seven minutes. I'm not sure just why I thought of that while I sat there waiting for Doug to arrive. It just seemed to register in my mind while I watched consumer after consumer get his or her food and leave.

I saw a large white pickup truck enter the parking lot from the eastward side of Highway 90. As he exited his truck, I could see that he was about 6'1" and weighed about 220 to 235 pounds. He carried under his arms a stack of papers. As he walked across the parking lot, each step that he took helped me to know that he was, in fact, the person that I was supposed to meet. His humble and delightful energy accompanied him to the door.

As he stepped inside, I stood up and smiled in his direction. I rose to meet him and extended my hand, not really fully aware of the opportunities for understanding that he would give to me. I didn't know that I was about to be presented with a treasure chest of knowledge which would accelerate my research of the history of the Katy Tigers football program.

From the very moment that we sat down and I turned on my recorder, he relayed detail after detail about a time period that only those who lived it would fully know. Doug was very organized with his presentation to me, as if he had always known that this day was going to happen and, in his eyes, the day was overdue. Doug no was longer a stranger.

He took me on a trip back to a time and place where I wanted to visit.

Working on the television series *Star Trek: The Next Generation* many years ago gave me a different perspective of time travel and just how easily the right set of circumstances could really take us there. Sure, we had the help of a great special effects man, Richard Mocksfield. This, however, was time travel of the purest kind.

There was no doubt that Doug had placed us both on the transporter station and hit the "Engage" panel the moment he sat down. All my pre-programmed questions seemed to fade away. Each moment had its question and answer. I was glad that the little recorder was capturing everything, for I could not write for being so caught up in the moment. "Here is a team roster of the players and coaches from the 1959 squad," he said, as my jaw dropped. Doug's name-by-name list of the players intoxicated me. His introduction of each young athlete was accompanied by a play-by-play of what he did on the team. The 12"x12" laminated team picture that he also presented me helped me to put faces to the names as we continued traveling through time.

For a moment, I flashed back to the first time that I saw the picture hanging on the upper wall over at Brookshire Brothers. This time, however, instead of looking up at the wall, I was looking down into my hands at an even closer look at the Tigers of 1959. Though dated in appearance, each player seemed to have that patented "proud-to-be-a-Katy-Tiger" look on his face. It was easy to see that, even back then, there was something extremely special about Katy, home of one of the best football programs in this nation.

Doug's father, like many in Katy at the time, worked at the local Humble Oil refinery. His mom, like most mothers of that time, stayed home to take care of the family. The television set was slowly making its way through American society at that time. Though most families did not have one, Doug told me that it was a common tradition on Friday evenings to gather at a home which did have a television set in order to watch everyone's favorite programs. He said that it was not uncommon to have ten or fifteen people sitting around a television set watching a program.

"On Sundays," he said, "church was never an option. If you were alive and walking, you were expected to attend church." However, it was the big after-church picnics that Doug seemed to look forward to the most. All of the Katy families joined together, each group bringing its favorite dishes.

"Gas prices were at an all-time high back then, topping an astounding 33 cents a gallon. Diesel was working its way upward to 18 cents a gallon. The average day at school started at 8:00 a.m. and ended around 3:30 p. m." Interrupting him, I asked him about the state of America at that time. "It was around the end of the cold war. Bomb shelters were the fad of the day, and teachers gave exercises weekly that helped kids prepare for the worst, should that day ever come. P.E. for the athletes was at sixth period, and practice went up until 5:30- 6:00 o'clock." One of the things that Doug remembered was that they did not have a weight room. Most of their exercises include resistance training, "...push-ups and pull ups, that sort of thing, accompanied by lots of drills."

When I asked Doug about the big game and what it was that he remembered the most, I saw his face settle back a calmness that made me feel that he was actually reliving his school life all over again. "What I remember the most about that time was the fact that many of us had never been away from our moms and dads before. Staying in a motel was a big-time deal for most of us. I hate to say it, but most of us had never been out of Katy before. So this was definitely a first for us back then."

"The papers had us as the big underdog back then. There were so many newspaper articles written about that game. But our coaches had us focused and well prepared for that game." Doug spoke of that time period with nothing less than great admiration. "It was a time that was soon to be the cornerstone of a foundation of excellence for Katy High football."

Doug and I sat at the small table as customers came and went. At on one point Doug took a look at his watch. We had been talking well over two hours. "I have my next appointment in about fifteen minutes." Before I could thank him for taking his time to share his stories with me, he said, "You know, I'm about to go to the wake of one of my old teammates Richard Fussell; you are more than welcome to join me if you like."

My first respond was that it was probably not a good idea; however, Doug was very genuine in his invitation. He said that there would be others present who played on the team with whom I could talk. I was still a little apprehensive. I had not planned my day to include a wake; those are the kinds of events for which you have to prepare yourself mentally. I asked him several more times, "Are you sure that I would not be intruding?"

"No, they are all good people. Come, you will see." There was no more resistance after that. I knew that when I started writing this book that its history would take me places that I never expected. The one thing I have learned over the years about being a writer is that I have to embrace the research process with an open mind and heart. If I don't, my readers will see it in my work.

As we drove up Highway 90, I could not help but remember something my mother used to say to us kids. "Make sure that you have on clean underwear, because you never know where you will end up." It never really made any sense back then, but suddenly it did right then!

Pulling up to Schmidt Funeral Home, I could see the cars parked all along side of the street. By this time I had lost all reservation of crashing the wake. Ironically, there was a movie out that week entitled *The Wedding Crashers*. This experience was actually about to happen to me. But, obviously, I knew the energy of happiness and excitement of a wedding was going to be absent.

Doug and I walked slowly up the sidewalk to the funeral home, and I began to feel the presence of sadness and loss reaching out and enveloping us as we approached the door. There was a small group of people gathered around a gentleman just outside the door. Doug quietly mentioned that he was Richard's brother. It was obvious that the brother was overcome with tremendous emotional loss. As I walked by him, I felt a part of my spirit reach over to embrace him.

At that same time I flashed back to the loss of my brother when I was eighteen. Though I did not know Richard's brother, my spirit knew that its purpose was to help ease his pain.

Doug stopped for a moment when he recognized another gentlemen coming out the door. Inside, the lobby was buzzing with activity and conversations. Small groups everywhere were sharing thoughts about life. Walking over to a group of about six people, Doug made his presence known. When he introduced me, I was happy to see that Charlie Shafer was one of those in the group. Charlie still maintained his same quiet demeanor from our meeting a few days before.

Charlie didn't realize it, but his presences helped to

make me feel comfortable about being there. Doug began to point out the players affiliated with the 1959 squad. Dwayne Fussell the quarterback of the team was the first whom I encountered after Charlie. When I first saw him, he was walking towards me: cowboy boots and big, silver belt buckle leading the way. When Doug introduced him to me, I could feel the confidence that accompanied him.

"Dwayne, this is Dexter Clay; he is writing about the history of Katy High School football." Dwayne reached out and shook my hand firmly. He seemed to be in control of his emotions. In fact, most of the people in the direct area of where Richard's body lay seemed to be surrounded by peace. In a way, they all seemed like they were celebrating the richness of Richard's life and not the days before his burial.

Dwayne was only in town for another twenty-four hours, so I did not want to ask him about being interviewed. Rather, I simply let him know about the *KatyNation* project and let him know that I would be contacting him. He did mention that he might be settling in at his mom's a little later and that he might have some time then. I passed him my card and said, "If, and only if, you feel up to it, feel free to call me. If not, I will contact you later."

After Dwayne walked back towards Richard's casket, I realized that Doug had been right. I did not feel out of place. It sounds strange but I felt like people I knew surrounded me. Just as that feeling settled into my heart, a young lady walked over to me and said, "Thank you for coming." She introduced herself as Richard's sister. I told her that I was so sorry about her loss.

She smiled politely and thanked me. I remembered thinking that she was in much more control of her emotions than her brother whom we encountered outside earlier. In fact, she moved around and worked the room, carrying herself with the grace of a sophisticated hostess at a very important social gathering.

I stood at the end of the center aisle, looking up towards where Richard's body lay. There were a number of people gathered there. Doug was off sharing thoughts with friends that he had encountered. I noticed Dwayne standing alone, looking over Richard's body. It was at this moment that I realized that I had seen the two together before. It was a few hours earlier, back at the restaurant where Doug and I had met. He had given me an old news clipping which posted an article featuring three young boys celebrating their State Championship title. The three boys were Charlie Shafer and Dwayne and Richard Fussell.

The impact of that moment weakened me briefly. I was allowed to see time gather all of us up and place us in a rare dimension of reality. Somehow, I found myself spiraling through a vortex which told me that I, too, was a part of this unfinished story. I felt that what I was searching for was not some mystical force which made Katy high football program so special. Rather, it was more of a powerful source that somehow made all those passing through Katy a part of one family.

My eyes caught the presence of an elderly man being helped into the back room. Later, Doug told me that he was Richard's father who was well into his 90s. You could see that his grief was as potent as that of his son whom I had passed earlier at the door.

Doug also pointed out Richard's mom and said, that after all the dust had settled, that I should try to talk with her about the book. He said that she was the team mother of their day and that she fed and kept order among the boys back then, as only a mother could. Even as she sat in her chair just a few feet from where her son's body lay, she carried a sense of order about herself.

Doug walked up and said, "You see that couple talking with Richard's mom? That is Coach Gordon Brown, and his wife Genevieve." I could not see him at first, for there were two people standing in my line of vision. But as they cleared out of the way, I saw two people who made a strong impact on me. My first thought was that they were royalty. Their presence made me understand why so many people were gathered around them. Coach stood as if he were the distinguished Senator of Texas, and his wife was, no doubt, the First Lady. Back in Los Angeles, I had been in the presence of great celebrities, but none whose first impression overwhelmed me like theirs.

Mrs. Brown's beauty was that of a cover girl. Sophisticated and elegant, she made me feel like Lauren Bacall or Grace Kelley was standing by Coach's side. "Hey are you ready to meet Coach?" Doug said a second time, interrupting my thoughts.

"Yes, sure, that would be great."

It was later that evening before I could log the events of the day in my journal. I had experienced a lifetime of Katy's history in one unscheduled event. The universe had said, "If you truly wanted to understand the history of Katy, you must become a part of its present."

After dinner that evening I decided to get my thoughts in order. I was not sure if I could actually capture the magnitude of such a powerful encounter.

"Coach Brown, I would like you to meet Dexter Clay. He is a writer, writing a book on the history of Katy High School football teams." Doug introduced me as I extended my hand. I felt no pretentious or arrogant energy from Coach Brown. What I felt was a spirit of humility. Of course I had to share my introduction with Coach with a few others who knew him. But his wife seemed to keep the conversation flowing whenever other admirers approached him.

If it is true that behind every successful man is a powerful woman, Genevieve was the poster child. When I told her how I got started with this project, she recognized my friend's name. Her face lit up with excitement. It appeared that she and Coach knew my friend and his wife very well. Her knowledge of my friends added a degree of worth to my project. I knew that I had to channel my desire to interview with Coach through his lovely wife. Coach was a celebrity who was constantly shaking hands with the other mourners.

"Well, Gordon rarely slows down these days. If you want a chance to interview him, your best bet is on the golf course." I had to smile inside, thinking that if he truly wanted to slow down, my golf game would literally put him to sleep. It was then that I felt I would someday have my moment with Coach Gordon Brown.

It was also then that my new friend Elnora walked up and shook hands with Coach and Genevieve. I stepped back to give her a chance to visit with her friends. I could see that Doug was about ready to leave. He asked me if I needed to stay longer.

That day was, in fact, one of those days that the universe had ordained as rewarding and fulfilling for me. Being a part of the final ceremonies of a man who was one of the Katy Tigers' first shining moments was nothing other than divinely planned.

Driving back towards my real world in Houston didn't seem to bother me that Saturday afternoon. It gave me time to contemplate the day.

I didn't know where the contacts that I had just made would take me. It was a direction I was anxiously awaiting to follow. I wondered just how I could get the community of

Katy to realize the magical nature of this land that they occupied. Then it dawned on me that the citizens must already know. However, this *KatyNation* story, rich in football heritage, somehow manifested itself in ways that most could not imagine.

I placed a called to Doug that evening; I wanted to thank him again for an incredible afternoon. Though unusual circumstances, I knew that I had been placed on the right path for researching this book. History and stories are often presented to us as generations of names and faces whom we rarely have a chance to verify. I was allowed to meet the faces and characters who helped to create the threads of fabric making up Katy Tiger football.

I wondered if the kids and parents of Katy's community today truly knew the extent of the tradition that they celebrate. I knew that they were excited about their winning football program, but I questioned if they really understood the source of their current success. I wanted to make a point to share with them the ingredients to that success.

From

Rice Field to Football Field
The Harold Andrews story.

"Many times, when passing by a cemetery, I have thought of the history that lies buried beneath many of the markers. For each of those individuals who reached adulthood before passing on, the events in their lives and their experiences would fill a book, and in many cases, several books. In the vast majority of cases, nothing is recorded of their lives, except their birth certificate, and in a relatively short span of years, nothing remains—their history has been vanished. I have thought of various individuals I have known who are now deceased, and I know that the story of their lives would have made interesting reading. But for one reason or another, it was never written.

"In recent years, the suggestion has been made for me to record some of my experiences. When I first considered the project, I felt that I really had nothing exceptional to write about; however, each life contains a history that is unique and completely different from any other. I think of the millions of individuals who lived and I've wondered about their childhood, their work, their pleasures, and adversities. Each one of millions would make an interesting book. So for what it's worth, here is my story.

"The account of my early years was written mainly for my immediate family; the later years are just for the record. I have told the stories from my personal point of view as I remember them, and I have no doubt that the siblings of our family will recall some of the events differently."

Harold Andrews
Author of *A Farmer's Life*
Katy Tiger football player pulled off of a rice binder in 1939.

I first heard the story the night of Katy's spring football game of 2006. It was from sportswriter and soon-to-be Editor of the *Katy Times,* Nick Georgandis. I saw Nick walking the sideline with a camera in his hands. As he came our way, Coach Gary Joseph, the current Head Coach of the Katy Tigers, introduced me to him. Coach let me know that if anyone had his hand on the pulse of the Katy football community, it was Nick.

Coach drifted off to address some other issues; Nick and I began to get acquainted. "If you are planning to write a book on Katy's football history," he said, 'the one thing that you will find hard to do is to maintain your course and stay focused. I say that to you because there are so many wonderful stories about this program that it is hard not to find yourself all over the place. If you can do this, you will find yourself in a pretty good place. This is truly a remarkable football community."

Nick began to share a few stories with me as we stood talking. Nick reminded me of Ray Romano on the old television show *Everybody Loves Raymond*. Plus, he looked like he could still put on a set of football pads if he had to do so. Nick mentioned a story to me that I thought would be the perfect opening to a movie, should this book ever get to the big screen.

He mentioned that there was a true story which involved one of the first coaches of Katy football not having enough boys to play. He eventually had to pull a kid off of a tractor in a rice field in order to fill out his team. I could see this up on the big screen. It was perfect. Nick continued, "I think that [the boy on the tractor] is living somewhere in Oklahoma. I'm sure that if you search around, you will find someone that knows how to reach him."

That was the first that I'd heard of Harold Andrews. Nick gave me his number and said that if I needed any help, he would be there for me and to call him anytime. My initial thought that this was too good to be a true story. I later found out that, like everything else about this *KatyNation* project, it too, was very real, and I was about to come face to face with Harold. Thanks again to Doug Gilbert who helped me to connect with Harold, I was about to live one of the oldest parts of Katy's football history.

Doug called me one afternoon with Harold's telephone number. I thanked him and anxiously awaited my opportunity to call Harold. I waited a couple of days before trying to contact Harold. I think that a lot of my success has to do with the fact that I like for things to have a natural course. When that happens, I don't have to worry about unsettling anyone. I prefer to wait a few days and compose myself. Another thing is that I found myself overly excited about this project. It is difficult to describe, but each contact that I made left me with a feeling that I was the captain of a ship that was set on autopilot, and my whole purpose on board was simply to enjoy the ride.

"Harold Andrews, please." This time someone answered. I had to leave a message on the first call.

"This is Harold." I was amazed at the strength that I heard in this man's voice.

"Hi, Harold, my name is Dexter Clay. I got your name and number from Doug Gilbert. How are you doing this evening?"

"Oh, I guess I'm doing pretty good. Nothing to complain about."

"Well, Harold, the reason that I'm calling is I heard that you were a part of the Katy football program back in 1939."

"Yes, yes, I was," he replied.

My heart started to race a little as I made that exciting trip back into time again. As a kid, I always enjoyed my history classes more than any other class. "Harold, as I left you in my first message, I am writing a book on the history of Katy High School. Harold, I sure would like to hear your story about life in Katy around the time that you were a student there."

"Well, I can tell you what I can remember about back then. I'm not really sure what day it was on, when they came out to the rice field to get me. I had been out in the rice field on the binder for a few hours when I saw the old black Ford coming up the small dirt road. This was kind of strange, something that you didn't see every day."

Interrupting him, "Now, Harold, you will have to pardon my ignorance, but what is a binder?"

"Oh! A binder is a machine that is pulled behind a tractor to cut the rice about ten or twelve inches above ground level. I believe its cutting area was about eight feet wide; the cut rice with heads attached falls back onto the 'table' of the binder, where a canvas type of belt transports it to a mechanical device that ties a certain amount into a bundle, with a string around it. Immediately, collection begins for the next bundle. The binder has a sort of basket that collects the bundles until it is loaded. The fellow on the binder has a handle for the job of raising or lowering the cutting blade for rice that is shorter or taller stocks.

"He also has a foot stirrup with which he can activate the basket of bundles, dropping them in a pile when he gets ready. On the next trip around the field, whatever he happens to have in his basket, he drops near the last drop of bundles. That way, the crew stands the bundles on end with the head up. It was not an impressive machine, but it was all we had to get the job done back then.

"As the dust settled behind the car, I could see two men and two boys getting out of the car and start walking over in my direction. I truly didn't know what to think at the time. So I just sat there on the binder with sweat rolling down my face.

"The first guy introduced himself as a school board member. I don't really remember his name. The other gentlemen said that his name was coach Ned Reader, the head football coach of the Katy Tigers. That was strange to me because I never remembered Katy even having a football team. 'Son we are putting together a football team and would like for you to play.' This was the fall of 1939. 'How about it? We will have to get your father's permission of course.'

"I was not really sure just how I felt at the time. It was kind of nice having these people coming all the way out here just to talk with me. I did not even think about the fact that I had never played the game of football before. You have to remember that we didn't have television back then. So we didn't even have a chance to know if we would like the game or not. I was surprised that my dad let me off to play football. But he was all for it. The next day I was a football player. There were not a whole lot of kids out there. After the first day of practice, I understood why.

"None of us were in football shape. Coach Reader had us doing all these different exercises, drills they called them, jumping up and down rolling across the ground like we had lost our minds. One of teammates was the Morton kid. We called him 'Boy,' that was his nickname. Boy's family owned a large farm in Katy. Heck, there were only seventeen kids in our whole senior class when we graduated back in 1941."

Once Harold started to talk, I didn't have to ask him many questions. He seemed to know that this was going to be a story one day. I could see the images of his past through his words as they came over the phone.

"Harold, did you know much about Coach Reader?"

"I don't have much information about Coach Ned

Reader, except what he told us. I feel sure that he did, indeed, play football at Baylor. He could have easily been a first-stringer, or he might have been one of the lesser ones who provided bodies for the varsity team to train against. But since that would have been some time before he was hired for our first football coach, most of us on Katy's first team would have been pretty young and probably were not paying much attention to college football. As I have said before, I doubt that any of the boys on our team had ever seen a real football game. Coach Reader was very plain spoken, and when he talked to the boys before practice, or during a game or at halftime, he had a booming voice, and he used it!

"His remarks were quite often a bit off-color as he made a point. But I liked him, and respected him. Looking back, I think he did a heck of a good job in developing a team from what he had to work with.

"We only had a week before school started to practice and try to learn and get in shape to play, and I thought I might die from a heat stroke. We always started our practice sessions with duck waddles, push-ups, running around the track, etc. Then came learning how to block and tackle. There were only six men on the field for each team; it took 15 yards to make a first down back in my day."

I asked Harold about the equipment back then. "I think that the kids today would really learn something from playing on a six-man team. I say that because, in many ways, especially on defense, it made you have to concentrate more. Most of the time, you found yourself face to face with the ball carrier. If you did not make the tackle, everyone would know that it was you that didn't make that tackle. So in a lot of ways, it made you maintain your focus at all times.

"I remember the helmets being pretty cheap back then. Any time that you took a direct hit, the helmets would cave in on the top pretty bad. I had a couple of helmets that would look like a train wreck by the end of the game.

"I never had much respect for those players who would always end up hurt all the time. Sure, it was a tough game, but some of the boys try to misuse being hurt. We used to call those kids 'grandstand players.' Don't get me wrong; I often would get up from a play with a headache. To me, the real challenge was to never let them see you hurt. Take an opponent's best shot and always get up. The toughest thing about our football uniforms was that they didn't get washed but once every week. Sometime those old uniforms would literally stand up by themselves!"

"So, what position did you play back then, Harold?"

"I started offense in the backfield, but I was just too light at 160 pounds. We had a few of the bigger boys who did better there. So, on offense, I finally found a home at right end. With such a small number of boys to pick from, we were really limited to those who had the ability and desire to play ball. Those of us on the first team had to play both offense and defense. On defense, our six-man team had three on the line, one roving backup (linebacker) right back of the linemen, and two in the backfield to protect against passes.

"On defense, I had the job of linebacker, and it seemed to me at that time I had to make more than my share of tackles. I know the other guys were doing their best, but that's just how six-man football is played. If the defensive lineman gets blocked out of the play, it's up to the linebacker to stop the runner. Of the other guys, just a few were suitable as substitutes. The rest of us had just better not get hurt! As I recall, very few really did get hurt during a game. Coach told us at various times that we should put out all we had, and we would not be as apt to get hurt. I believe that was true. The first year, my jersey number was #2. The second year it was

#24. At that time, the number meant nothing to me, just a number. Ned Reader was only at Katy High for a year, and then after that, Thomas Smitherman was our coach.

"Katy High had four senior boys that year who were all fair sized. Junior Lummus, whose father worked for Houston Light and Power at the plant out west of town, was the heaviest and had the most drive through the line. Not real fast, but he sure jolted me when we practiced, and I had to tackle him! His knees just made every fiber of my body ache!

"Jesse Bruton was the fastest runner we had and the tallest. He could have made the first string of any team. I can't recall which one was the quarterback the first year, I think that it was Floyd, he player quarterback or center. Too many years have passed. Ray Ginn was the quarterback the second year and was an excellent passer. Also, he was a smart guy, being near the top of the class all the time.

"The other two seniors, (both near 200 pounds) were Floyd Haskett and Wesley Buller from Pattison. Floyd was a strong player for us that first year. I may be wrong, but I believe Floyd has a son in the Katy School system. All four of those guys had the heart to play ball.

"Our first game, we got beat 50-6. In fact, we lost every game that year except for the last one. Our coach, Ned Reader was kind of a tough old guy. I'm not really sure just how many of the guys really liked him. Since he was the only coach that we had back then, I just kind of learned how to deal with him. Today, kids have a coach for basically every position. It wasn't that way back in my day. Yeah, we did not have any assistant coaches back in the day.

"As far as football field was concerned, on its best day it was in pretty poor condition. Filled with grass burrs all over the place, it was simply better to be on your feet than to be down on the ground. That first year was pretty tough. We lost to every team that we played, except for the last game. Yes, we did manage to win the last game of the season. That was pretty nice. I remember how excited the whole town was after that first victory. It was as if no one even remembered the terrible losses that we had before that win.

"Now that I look back on it, even when we lost, the whole town was still always behind us. Katy was such a small town back then. However, the townspeople were still always out there to see us play. In fact, to this day I can still remember the voice of a Katy fan shouting out my name from the stands. I never knew who he was, but I can still hear his words of encouragement, 'Great job Harold! Good hit Harold!'

"Today, Katy has thousands of fans that come out to see them play. Though we had much smaller numbers, they were still as excited about Katy High School football as they are today."

"Harold, this is such beautiful information that you are sharing with me. Do you remember much about your locker rooms back then?" I'm not sure why I asked that question. It was just that Harold's description of things was so vivid that I could see clearly what his past looked like.

"Our locker room wasn't very big, with three or four shower heads in the shower. Hot and dark, and of course steamy in there, as I recall. The thing that stands out in my mind about that dressing room was the smell of sweat after practice. We wore the same uniforms all week before they got cleaned, and they got pretty 'ranky'! They were usually cleaned before each game, so they looked pretty good then. By the end of the week, those uniforms could literally stand up by themselves.

"When we suited up for practice each day, those jerseys were still wet from the day before and it took several minutes to get used to that ugly feel!"

"What about your principal back then?"

"I don't think we had a person in the school system with the title, 'Principal.' The superintendent handled all the administrative duties. The superintendent during my junior year was Jesse Fox. He was only there for a year and was replaced by D. H. Blackmon, who also was the high school English teacher. I thought a lot of Mr. Blackmon, both as a person and also one who could really teach English. A young fellow of the community was killed in a tractor accident, and I still recall the beautiful song that Mr. Blackmon sang at that funeral.

"Did I tell that I am restoring a 1955 two-door hardtop Century Buick? Doris and I bought one just like this one in the fall of 1954 when that model first came on the market. At that time, we had two small boys. Little boys are sometimes mischievous, and the younger of them, Douglas, had the bright idea of putting sand in the gas tank of that car. It was quite an ordeal to get the fuel system completely clean again! We will never let him forget that!"

"When did you move from Katy?" I asked.

"We moved to Oklahoma in the spring of 1973, after quitting the rice farming business and raising cattle from high school days until that time. When we moved to Oklahoma, I intended to just raise cattle, so we acquired 500 mother cows with calves. The cattle market broke that year, so we decided to diversify. We had good red river bottomland, and we started farming wheat, soybeans, and alfalfa hay. Also, we reduced the cattle herd and started an artificial insemination program, breeding to sell Simmental bulls at two years of age. That proved to be a good move, and now we see the Simmental influence in various cattle herds around Idabel to which we sold bulls."

"Wow, Harold, you have certainly had an exciting life."

"Yes, I have been very blessed. You know, I started building my first airplane, a GLASAIR, on my 60th birthday, 1984. It required three and a half years to complete it. One year of that time was probably used to bring it up to show quality. And then, I was fortunate to win an Outstanding Workmanship Award at the big annual Sport Airplane Show at Oshkosh, Wisconsin, in 1989. As I built the plane, I wanted it to be good enough to compete, but I never dreamed that it would actually win!

"Then, after a few years, having no real need for the plane, we sold it. That was around 1992. A wealthy family in Florida still has the plane, and I understand the grandson of the fellow who bought it wants to keep it forever! I'm pleased. The fellow and his wife in Florida who wound up with it are both deceased.

"After that, I figured my flying days were over. But as the end of the decade approached, I began to have second thoughts and decided to build another. It would not be the '200 mph' kind like the first one but would be very lightweight with a slow take-off and landing speed. By the time I got it finished, I had had open-heart surgery and had gotten a pig valve installed! Couldn't get a license to fly then, so I did the maiden flight, (without a license!) and added sixty more hours! With my heart problem, we decided it would be wise to sell it. I never did like that little plane, even though it fulfilled the design criteria of the people who made the kit. The quality was nowhere close to the first airplane."

"Wow, Harold!" I was trying to write down everything that I was hearing as fast I could!

"You know, I once wrote a book about my early days in Iowa and my folks moving to Katy, Texas. I called it *A*

Farmers Life. It even had some early pictures of what Katy looked like back in 1936." Before I could say another word he said, "I think that I might have the last copy of that lying somewhere around here. If you promise to get it back to me, I will mail it out to you."

"Why, sure Harold," I said. "It is very considerate of you to even offer it."

Somewhere along the way, it had been written in the stars that this book and the countless people who actually live it and I were supposed to cross paths. It was this kind of cosmic energy that helped to keep me on course and focus in the completion of *KatyNation*.

It was a few weeks later, when I received a package in the mail from Harold Andrews. Ironically enough, it came at the same time that I received a letter from Coach Gordon Brown. Inside Harold's package was the last original copy of his book *A Farmers Life.* I felt privileged to have had received it. Perusing the book, I was brought face to face with the reality of what Katy, Texas, was like in her early years.

I didn't know if Harold realized it or not but the cover of the book had a hand-drawn picture of a young boy driving a tractor pulling some type of harvesting machine not far behind. Could this be the famous binder that Harold was once extracted from to play the game called football? Inside the book, Harold had sent me a couple of pictures of what Katy looked like the year he and his family arrived. In fact, a couple of those old building can still be found in Katy today.

A colored photo of Harold's last plane was also included. When you think of someone having the knowledge to build an airplane, you think of an aerodynamics expert. You don't think of a farmer from Katy, Texas. But during my research for this book, I kept finding that Katy's history was enriched with men and women who learned not to place limits on what they could accomplish.

After Harold shared with me the name of one of his teammates, Floyd Haskett, I remembered that there was a gentleman by the name of Bill Haskett who was still a member of Katy ISD. So, it was his door that I wanted to knock on next. It was at that time in my life that I decided to place all my other projects on hold. I had been trying to remodel my house and tie up some loose ends on a couple other things. I was beginning to feel responsible for the completion of this book.

I started to feel that there were a lot of people out there, both young and old, who needed to know more about their history. They needed to know the quality of the people living in this community was no accident. There were many elder statesmen out there who had cleared the way for the success of today's Katy Tigers.

Three Times a Tiger

Franz Family

Anyone who has ever driven through Katy at one time or another has come across Franz Road. It is one of the few roads which profile Katy's past, present, and future. Some sections are lined with acres of endless pastures and an occasional cow or two. Some stretches boast grand, new subdivisions with paved streets and community parks for kids to play. There are also large, vacant lots with only small billboards preparing passers by for the buildings of the future.

To most of those in Katy, Franz Road is more than a street name; it is a reminder of those who lived in a time when Katy was still young. If a person ever wanted to learn something about Katy's history, he wouldn't have to look very far. Just walk up to anyone and ask.

I was on the sidelines of a Katy playoff game in 2006, when I ran into the real history of Franz Road. I didn't know it at the time, but the Katy mom with whom I was talking on the sidelines happened to be a member of the Franz family. Mrs. Franz led me to an interview that I will always remember as she shared with me that her father-in-law Raymond played for the 1955 Tigers, her husband Kevin played for the 1980 Tigers, and her son Kolby was a part of the current 2006 Katy Tiger team.

A few days later, I contacted Kevin and asked him if there was a possibility that I could meet with him and his father. I had a feeling that it would be an interview that I would enjoy. The Franz family has an office located a little behind the Texas Tradition restaurant in Katy. This would be our meeting place early Thursday morning. You never really appreciate a generation until you see three members from the same family standing in front of you at one time.

The Franz's secretary Sharon Walton greeted me with a big smile when I walked into the front door. I soon met Kevin and his younger son Kyle for the first time. Grandfather Franz was just pulling up. Inside the front office was a picture that included members of the early Katy community: the faces of Kevin's grandfather, Dr. Bing, A.O. Miller, and several other dominant community figures adorned the wall.

Kevin took me into his father's office to show me a composite of three pictures of him, his brother and his father standing next to three different champion steers. You can never realize how magnificent a steer can be until you see a champion steer.

Kevin remarked, "L.D. Robinson put together the agriculture program [for Katy] which was modeled through the state."

Still holding the large, framed picture in his hands, his younger son Kyle asked, "Is that you, Dad?"

With a large proud smile on his face, Kevin replied, "Yes, this is me."

We walked back to the conference room where Raymond Franz joined us. I knew that he carried with him the knowledge of the city of Katy. "Mr. Franz, how long have you lived in Katy?"

"I was born in Katy some sixty-nine years ago. I graduated from Katy High School back in 1955. Back in my day, we were such a small town. I don't think that the school was even Class A at the time. We were what they called Class B. Schools went from first grade to twelfth grade.

"This used to be only rice and cattle community.

Today, all the rice elevators are shut down. There are none of them operating today."

"I never really understood the rice elevators. Was that a process that they used to cure the rice?"

"You harvest the rice in the field. It has about 20% moisture still in it, so it has to be dried. All these tall elevators that you still see around here at one time had farmers fighting to get in line to get their rice dried."

His son, Kevin, added, "This 2006 crop year was the first year that none of the rice dryers in Katy were operating. Back in the '70s, there was some 70,000 acres of rice going through the dryers here in Katy. Last I heard, they we were down to around..." he looked at his dad.

Raymond said, "...were down to about seven or eight thousand acres."

Kevin continued "That's what kept all those rice dryers busy back then. So 2005 was the last year that we were in operation."

Raymond said, "In addition to that, we also had about 50,000 acres of soy beans being dried for a while here, but that didn't last very long. It used to be that you could ride from here to Waller and visibly see those rice fields all along the road. Today, they have been replaced with subdivisions.

"It doesn't seem that long ago, but I remember when I-10 was two lanes. There was not very much going on between here and Houston. Property was most of the farmers' salvation, economically. If you owned your property and could hold on to it, it would eventually pay off for you, and you could salvage something out of it."

"Mr. Franz, do you remember a lot about your father?'

Raymond answered, "Oh yes, he was born right here in Katy. He is the one that the road was named after."

Kevin continued, "From what I understand, some of the original family homesteads, back in the middle 1800s, were back around where Franz and Mason Road meet."

He trailed off as Raymond talked, "Dad farmed peanuts until 1947. He had three hundred acres of peanuts where Wal*Mart is back towards the west. He said that year it rained so much that he could not even dig for the peanuts. The crop was a total loss, so the next year he realized, with all the water, that it was better that we farmed rice. So, we drilled a well on my granddad's place. His name was Chris, and his wife was named Emma. Emma's family was on the dairy side of farming. My granddad had a twin brother back then named Pete Franz. But Pete was not a farmer. There were about seven children in that family.

"Anyway in 1953, my dad sold about a 100 acres of land here and bought about five hundred up towards Hockley. That was during my sophomore year. During the later part of the season, I had to ask my mother to take me out to catch a bus. Then by my senior year, I got the family's '54 Mercury to drive to school. But I had to milk three cows in the morning, and by the evening after football practice, even though it might be dark, I had to bring those cows in to milk them again."

Picture of 1955 Squad

Raymond Franz bottom row third from the right.

I had to laugh to think that kids gripe about having to take the trash out these days.

"Mr. Taylor allowed me to continue to go to school at Katy, even though we were in the Waller School District. Well, Dad served on the school board of Katy.

"We were living around Barker back then. I was probably about sixth or seventh grade when they consolidated with Addicks School District. All of the seventh graders moved over to Katy. It was a big controversy back then. Half of the school board wanted to the kids to go to Spring Branch, the other half to Katy. Thank goodness that Katy was our better choice. My dad and Mr. Taylor did a lot of work to get things to move towards Katy. Mr. Taylor really was a fine fellow. Anyway, there was not but twenty-four kids in high school at the time at Addicks. When we came to Katy, when we graduated, we had forty kids in our graduation class. That was the largest class that had ever graduated at Katy by 1955."

He pulled out two old yearbooks from Katy in 1954 and 1955. I could sense his nostalgia for the time period and felt my own heart leap a couple of beats when I saw the scratches that covered the face of the old maroon manuals. I turned the pages slowly so I wouldn't damage them.

"Wow, look at this!" The first thing that I came across was a dedication to Mr. James E. Taylor and a picture of him. It was the first time that I had seen the face of the man of whom I have been reminded constantly for his contributions to the Katy community. Captured in his smile was the face of a humanitarian whose mission was to serve his fellow man.

The inscription underneath the picture said it all: "He has counseled with us and assisted us, understood our problem - An avid fan of all school activities, he has encouraged clubs and organizations, enhancing our chances for success - His devotion to the schools and its programs has brought extensive development and notable achievements. As an expression of our appreciation for his many contributions, the annual staff dedicates the '55 Tiger Echo to Mr. James E. Taylor, our Superintendent."

It was easy to see why people in Katy admired this person. Both Kevin and I were excited about seeing his father in the book. I think that it was his first time to view the old yearbooks as well. I quickly rustled through my briefcase to find my glasses.

Raymond pointed to a picture of two young ladies in the book. "There's the twins. My wife was one of the twins. Her dad was...."

Kevin interrupted, "That was A.O. Miller. My

grandfather was the twins' dad that I was telling you about in the picture earlier."

"Oh I see, wow, this really brings things to life now."

Raymond added, "Joan made up three generations of the Katy High School band. She was in the band, her granddaughter is in the band."

"Ok, now, this is Joan Miller, who is Joan Franz now, and her sister is Jean."

Turning the pages to get to the sports section, all three of us were enjoying our walk down memory lane. There it was, the Katy Tiger football team of 1955. There were pictures of Head Coach Ralph McCord and Fred Ruland.

Kevin said, "Oh, Fred Ruland was still a teacher at Katy when I was in school."

Underneath the pictures of the two coaches was the squad. You couldn't see their jersey numbers like you can today in sports photographs.

I read the names out loud: "David Baker, Jack Bierman, Blevins Bundick, Paul Carroll, John Culpepper, Thomas Guzman, Jerry Egger, Donnie Faulk, Dale Faulk, John Fry, Douglas Freeman, John Fisher, Raymond Franz, Frank Garcia, Julius Gibbs, John Goynes, Loyd Hall, Floyd Hall, Douglas Harrel, Glen Lewis, Edd Longenbaugh, Dennis McKeon, George Miller, Buzzy Miller, Wayne Pearson, Jack Rhoads, Jimmy Sparks, Reed Smith, Billy Spencer, Alton Sturm, Albert Thompson, John Scott West, Billy Don Williams, James Woods, and Leroy Doss."

There they were, the names and faces of Tigers past, immortalized on two pieces of paper. I watched Kevin smiling over the picture of his father in his uniform and could not help but feel that it was a very special moment for all of us in that room. We were looking back into a part of history that will never really have a chance to say anything again, unless someone from the future reaches back to give it a voice. As Mr. Franz turned the pages, between two pages was an old black and white photograph of the 1955 team wearing full pads. It was a picture that did not need words because it spoke for itself.

On the next page, we found Mr. Franz again, this time on the track team. Kevin said, "Dad actually went on to high jump up at Sam Houston as well."

Raymond remarked, changing the subject, "Though they didn't have our scores in that annual, I think the first five games of that season, nobody every scored on us. We played Pasadena B, who was a much larger school than we were."

"Mr. Franz, what do you think that you weighed back then?"

Raymond replied, "Oh, probably 150 or 160 pounds. We did not have any big guys back then. Our biggest guy was probably about 180 pounds. The 300 pound kids did not exist back then."

"I know what you mean. I think today they call the offensive line the Hogs here today at Katy. They are pretty impressive.

"Well I was a guard at 160 pounds. Back in my day, we tried to make up for size with a little speed. If we lined up against someone that was larger than we were, then we just understood that we had to hit them harder, that's all!"

We laughed out loud. "Hey, I guess that is true. I did not think about it that way, but it makes sense."

"In fact, we used to enjoy hitting those big guys, just to see what kind of noise that they would make. Johnny Fisher was my close friend back then. He was right guard, and I was left, and Herman Myers, who today was over at Midway Grocery, was the center. Herman was the most athletic kid in these annuals."

"It's a funny, you don't think of the center being the most athletic kid on the football field. Today, you think of the quarterback or halfback, or maybe a linebacker, but you don't think of a center being the best athlete on a team. When you do stop to think about it, it is the center that starts off the whole progression of the game."

"We had great agriculture programs back then as well. Both of the boys, Dale and Kevin, had Champion Steers back then."

"Yes, Kevin showed me the pictures back in your office."

We continued to move through the annual and came across a picture of the school board. Gathered around a solid oak table sat A. J. Mangum; A. W. Thompson; D.E. Elder, Vice President; C. D. Gordon, President; C. I. Cardiff, Secretary; J E. Taylor, Superintendent; G. L. Short, Treasurer; and M. L. Scott. They were all names that were synonymous with Katy's growth, but I'm sure they were names that many had forgotten over the years, unless of course, there were schools named after them.

Even if some of these names were forgotten, they are still embedded in the foundation of Katy Independent School District's continued quest for excellence.

I could hear in the background that the Franz's next appointment had arrived. Quite honestly, I believe that we could have talked all day long about their lives. It is a rarity to come across four generations of a family that still resides in one community. I guess they knew what was special about this community that makes people want to stay around. There is no doubt that a strong family bond is one of the principle keys to building a powerful community.

I stopped by the front office to say goodbye to Sharon, who had been so nice to copy some pages from the annuals so that I could have the correct spelling on the players' names from Raymond's 1955 team. Also, I could see Kevin's family pride for being in the center of a family that allowed him to know the power of his heritage and his future, all at the same time. Through the eyes of the Franz family, I was given a taste of the past, the present, and the future of Katy football program.

Katy's rich tradition is easy to understand when you meet a family like the Franz family who has helped to plant the seeds which give life to their community. Katy is filled with families like the Franz's. When the Tigers take the football field, their opponents are not playing against the students in front of them. In a roundabout way, they are playing against the sons of Katy and the fathers of Katy and the grandfathers of Katy.

A Name to Remember

Haskett

The more I researched the history of Katy High School football, the more I was handed names of people who helped build this program. I was gathering pieces to a puzzle that had been lying around this community for years. I questioned why no one had taken the time before to put these pieces together.

There are countless names embedded in the heart of Katy that seemed to be quietly interesting, waiting for a book to be written to give them a chance to be remembered. The last name "Haskett" was becoming a loud echo. The first time I heard the name was from Coach Joe Bright. Then I heard it from Coach Mike Johnston.

The importance of the name did not register until I heard it from Harold Andrews. I asked Harold if he had remembered many of the guys who played on his team. He said he did not remember them very well.

"I do remember Floyd Haskett. He had two brothers; he was our quarterback. I remember him because he was the kind of player that always gave it a hundred percent on the field. You always knew that Floyd was ready to play. He was the kind of player that made you want to play harder. In fact, I think that he has a son that is still in the Katy School District."

This is when the light bulb over my head tipped over

and knocked me a couple of times. "Hello, is anybody home? Haskett, Bill Haskett, could he be the son of the quarterback that Harold spoke of in one of his emails to you?" Okay, I must admit sometimes those pieces to life's puzzles are lying so close to us that it is very easy to walk right over them.

It was not very hard to locate Bill. In my conversation with Coach Bright that you will read later, he told me that Bill Haskett who worked for Katy ISD was a very good friend of his. So, it took only one phone call to the Katy district office to find Bill. "Hello, Bill, my name is Dexter Clay. I am writing a book called *KatyNation*."

"*KatyNation* is the first of two books about the history and success of the Katy High School football program." I told him that I had heard from Harold Andrews that his father Floyd Haskett was on the first team back in 1939.

"Yes, yes he was."

"Bill, my reason for calling is in hopes to interview you to find out a little bit more about your dad and his days in Katy football."

"Well sure, I can tell you what I remember about my father's football days. When did you want to meet?"

"Any time that it is convenient for you, Bill."

"Well, let's see, early next week will be fine. We can meet here at the office."

"Bill, that will be great. How does Tuesday sound?"

"Sounds good to me. Let's say 11:00."

"That will be perfect. Thank you so much for your time." I hung up the phone. I'm not sure why I get so excited when I hang up the phone from scheduling an interview with a person. Maybe it is because I know that deep down inside, that the greatest gift that your fellow man can give you is the gift of his or her time. It was Friday afternoon when I placed that call to Bill. So, I anxiously waited to get his thoughts about his father Floyd Haskett.

Tuesday morning came; I found myself traveling west on Clay Road again. Turning left on Fry Road, I took it up to Interstate 10 towards Katy and the Katy ISD central office. The central office didn't really look like a workplace. It seemed so clean and organized. The first thoughts that came to mind were that Katy had come a long way from the farmhouse classrooms of its beginning. At a center counter, I greeted two ladies. "Good morning, my name is Dexter Clay. I have an eleven o'clock appointment with Bill."

"Okay, Bill's office is 1610, down the hall on the right."

"Thank you," I said, heading down the hall. I remembered thinking to myself that it was kind of nice to see that whoever designed the building had created a mixture of corporate office and school atmosphere. It created a very warm and peaceful workplace.

Ha! 1610. I opened the door and walked up to the receptionist. After I introduced myself, she pointed to Bill's office on the right. Looking over my right shoulder, I saw two men standing in the office with a glass front. Bill greeted me at the door.

"Dexter, I want you to meet my brother Floyd."

"Wow, Floyd, so you were named after your father!" I said out loud. For the first few minutes of the meeting, I introduced Bill and Floyd to what *KatyNation* was all about and let them know to where and with whom my research had taken me thus far. "So far, I have Interviewed Harold Andrews, Coach Gordon Brown, Mike Johnston, and Coach Joe Bright. I have also gathered thoughts from many in the community of Katy."

I wanted them to know that the *KatyNation* project was not just a human-interest article but also something that was going to be published and distributed throughout the country. I explained to the two brothers that I was going to have to do this project in two books, past and present, because of the overwhelming history of the community and the Katy High School program. I told them that I thought it was necessary to understand the history of any successful program.

"This is my approach for this book." I said. "I will show the passing of the torch to Coach Joseph and start *KatyNation2* about his legacy and the future of Katy High School football." I added that, after the first book, I would finish the screenplay because I felt this story had the potential to be a movie someday. When I heard myself sharing these thoughts, I suddenly realized that I was laying out the foundation and the blueprint for my future. The excitement from the blessing of writing this book almost overwhelmed me.

I had to force myself to focus on why I was there. "So, how many children were in your father's family," I asked, directing the first question towards Bill.

"Three boys and one girl. The youngest son did play football for Katy. His name is Martin. He was a pretty good player. Katy was either 1A or 2A."

Floyd then spoke up. "Katy was 2A at the time."

Then Bill said, "It was '62 through '65; he played four years. Martin was all-district all four years."

It was interesting to be interviewing two people at the same time.

"Like a lot of kids back then, Martin played both ways. On the original team, you had to play both ways because there were only sixteen kids on the team," added Floyd.

Bill commented, "As a freshmen Martin made

honorable mention; he was pretty good linebacker and receiver."

"Your dad played on the six man team. Did he ever talk about that at all?" I asked.

He continued, "A little bit about some of the places that they had to go like Weimer High School. He said that they didn't want to get out of bounds because the grass burs were so bad that they would jump all over your shoe strings and socks. I understand that, that was the big challenge in that day. Football fields were in pretty bad condition back then."

Floyd said, "Dad mentioned that the equipment was pretty sparse back then as well. Very little protection in the shoulder pads. The thigh pads were very small, of course they had the old leather helmets." The fact that their father actually wore one of those old leather helmets made me smile.

I added, "Can you imagine taking the kind of hits that we see today, while wearing only one of those old leather helmets? I remembered Harold Andrews saying that his helmet would cave in all the time. You almost would have to have had an animal mentality to play in the equipment back then. It was a different ball game."

Bill said, "You had to think about this. At least here in Katy my dad's situation, as well as the fifteen others that played with him...they didn't have weight rooms and stuff. Most of them back then were these small skinny kids. I think that my dad was pretty lightweight. I mean he put on weight as he got older, but in school, for the most part, I think that he was pretty lightweight. I guess that whatever muscular physique that he had was from growing up on the farm."

"Was it a family farm that your dad lived on?"

Bill replied, "Actually Dad lived over in Brookshire. His family had a farm over there. They farmed a little of everything. Corn, watermelon, and cotton. Most of the guys from around here were from off the farms.

"Something you just reminded me of when you said 'different ball game,' back in my father's day after a touchdown was scored back, for the extra point, you had to drop kick the football between the goal post, instead of using a kicking tee."

"Wow that's amazing!" I said. "That had to have taken a lot of talent, especially when you had players coming at you, too!"

Floyd answered, "Yes. The ball had to touch the ground first before you could kick it. When we were kids and we would play, that was the way that we played the game, as well. In those days, everybody played both ways. Our dad was a quarterback."

"You know, I have to tell you this. Harold Andrews said that your father was the kind of player that you could count on. To me as an ex-athlete, the greatest compliments always came from my teammates. They always knew if you were giving it your all or not. That is the one thing that he did mention about your father."

Floyd remarked, "I was talking just before you came in, Dexter, about my father. He didn't ready talk much about it, but I don't think that he had ever seen a football game before. Maybe you listened on the radio. By then, you went to the movies, and they would have clips, maybe of football. I don't think that they had very much to relate football to."

"That's so true because television came out in the late forties."

"That's about right. So they would not have had the opportunity.

"Talking about equipment, I think the players had to furnish their own shoes; the teams furnished the helmet pads and jerseys." He handed me an 8"x10" sheet of paper. "This

is from the first football team that was out of the yearbook."
It was a copy of a picture from the 1939 yearbook of the Katy
Tigers' squad. Like a little kid, I was in awe of the picture.

"Wow, this is great! We have to get a picture of this
for the book. Do you have the original to this?"

"My sister has the original of this. I don't know if the
high school has a copy of this or not." "I was not going to put
a lot of pictures in the book, but there were a few that I
thought would really be nice to insert. This is one of them."

Floyd continued, "We were laughing about the
originality of the numbering system on their jerseys. They
only had sixteen players, so the numbering is one through
sixteen." We all laughed at Floyd's observation.

Bill added, "One of the guys that played on that first
team, I think that it might have been Jesse Bruton...well, at a
reunion a number of years later, he told me that he was in the
Air Force in World War II. He said that he wore his school
football cleats inside his bombardier boots to help keep his
feet warm."

"Oh, that is a great story. I hope that we can get a
copy of this for the book. It sort of speaks for itself. You look
at this picture, and you look at a photo of today of the 150
kids that roam the sidelines, and you realize just how far this
program has come."

"Yes, you look at that bottom paragraph. It talks about
the Dads' Club purchasing $250.00 dollars worth of
equipment for the team."

"Oh, that is so true. You think of how much money
the boosters donated to the program today."

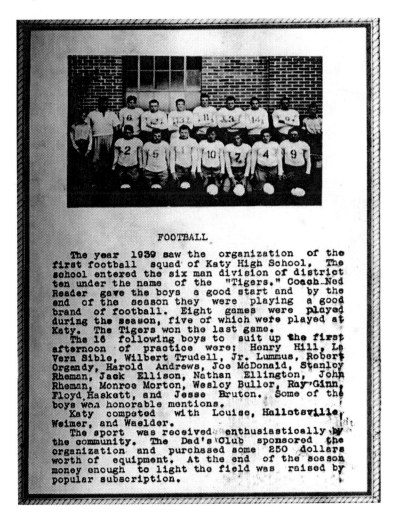

FOOTBALL

The year 1939 saw the organization of the first football squad of Katy High School. The school entered the six man division of district ten under the name of the "Tigers." Coach Ned Reader gave the boys a good start and by the end of the season they were playing a good brand of football. Eight games were played during the season, five of which were played at Katy. The Tigers won the last game.

The 16 following boys to suit up the first afternoon of practice were: Henry Hill, Le Vern Sible, Wilbert Trudell, Jr. Lummus, Robert Organdy, Harold Andrews, Joe McDonald, Stanley Rheman, Jack Ellison, Nathan Ellington, John Rheman, Monroe Morton, Wesley Buller, Ray Ginn, Floyd Haskett, and Jesse Bruton. Some of the boys won honorable mentions.

Katy competed with Louise, Hallotsville, Weimer, and Waelder.

The sport was received enthusiastically by the community. The Dad's Club sponsored the organization and purchased some 250 dollars worth of equipment. At the end of the season money enough to light the field was raised by popular subscription.

First Katy tiger Team 1939

Floyd said, "It looks like that picture was taken outside where the old high school used to be. I think that Katy Elementary School is sitting on that site today. It was there until the fifties, I guess, before they moved it."

"They talked about, how at lunch time, they would get an hour for lunch. Many of the kids walked home for lunch," added Bill. One piece of information that I want to share with the readers of this book is about the support of the Booster Club. I guess that, technically, it would have formed out of this Dad's Club. Wow, so the dads were actually involved back then!

It's funny, we always think of mothers being the ones supporting the school programs. Today, both mothers and fathers go the extra yard to support their children's school programs.

Floyd remarked, "I know that they had a band back then; I don't know if they had a pep squad. Our mother was a year behind our dad in high school. Her name at the time was Alice Christiansen. I can remember her talking about catching the old school buses coming up the old gravel roads back then."

Bill handed me another copy and said, "I don't know if you have a copy of this. This is a copy of a letter that Harold sent to an alumnus named Judy back in 2004. I'm sure that he has shared those things with you already." By quickly reading through the letter, I could tell that Harold had shared everything on it with me already.

I said to them, "You know, it is so obvious that Harold has such a love for being a part of the Katy football program. You can actually hear the passion in his voice as he speaks about Katy today. It is a very unique thing here in Katy. I have not come across anyone who has been negative about this football community. I mean, I'm sure that Katy's opponents would beg to differ. But here in this community, everyone that I have come across has been so positive.

"When you talk about Katy High School football, the

community here gets so excited. They want to tell you their
story, tell you their kids that have played in the program. I
first thought to myself 'This is too unreal.' It was like the
movie with the Stepford wives; everything seemed too
perfect, as if things had been scripted."

Bill replied, "It was kind of unusual that Dad and
Mom both graduated from Katy. My brothers, sister and I all
graduated from Katy. Now, even our children have graduated
from Katy."

"Even on Mother's side, our grandmother, even
though she didn't go to school here, lived here about a 100
years ago. Her younger brother is still living here in Katy. I
know that is not part of your story, but he would tell us that
showing off in those days was being able to ride your horse to
school," continued Floyd. We all laughed. "That was back
probably in the 1930s."

"That really puts it into perspective, doesn't it?" I
replied.

I found myself talking more in this interview than
most of the others. I'm not sure why. These two brothers who
had taken their time to help educate me about Katy's history
had unconsciously put in perspective some of the things that I
had been searching for. I was getting a crash course right then
and there about the Katy community.

This is a community about family and the extensions
of family. I was starting to believe that football was merely
an extension of the family activities that had been blessed by
a very powerful source.

Countless thoughts were racing through my mind
while I sat in Bill's office. It occurred to me that it might be
easy in most in this community to forget its humble
beginnings. Today, it is easy to lose sight of the fact that one
hundred years ago, Katy High started out as a very small high

school. "Bill, how many high schools does Katy have today?"

"Katy has six schools, over fifty thousand students. When I was in high school, maybe there were 300 kids, total."

Floyd said, "When I was in high school there were fifty three people in my graduating class. I graduated in 1960 and Bill in '61."

"We have been here long enough to see that a lot of these subdivisions being built, were once rice fields that we work in. New homes are now located in areas where dairy farmers lived," Bill added.

Floyd said, "It's had to put your finger on it, because it was basically a farming community. I think about the things that could have prevented it from being a community, even the time that we were growing up. I think that the population of the community was about 630 for years. However, with that population, I bet we had eight or ten different churches. There are a couple of things that I felt kept this community together. One it was the school, not just football, but things related to school. The other thing that was very big around here at that time was the agriculture-type thing.

"In that, is a whole other story about the livestock and rodeo that got started back here. It actually got started on the football field at Katy High. It was the first in Texas, or could have been the first in the nation."

"Oh, Coach Brown gave me a copy of a movie that was shot here called…."

Bill smiled, "*Tom Boy and Champ.*"

"Yes that it!"

Floyd said, "We were both in the opening scene of that movie. We were in the scene where the band came marching up the street in the parade."

"Hey, I remember that scene, and I wondered if that was Katy's High School Band."

Bill answered, "Well, a couple of things in that movie were special for us. The feed store that you saw in the movie was where our dad worked. The arena that they were using in the movie was the old gymnasium from the old high school. Back in 1959 when Katy went to state, they had a special on TV about the city of Katy closing down. It showed a caravan of cars leaving town to go to the game."

"I had heard that before," I said to Bill. "Now, you guys were at that game?"

"Yes, the band played at halftime."

Floyd said, "Bill was the Principal of Katy for what, fifteen years, 1981 through '96."

"Then Bill, you have had a real opportunity to see this community form, being right in the heart of it," I said.

"Yes, I have. Today, I announce many of the football games, and it is kind of embarrassing when we play schools like Alief and Elsik. Here's Katy with four thousand people in the stands, and the other school has only three hundred or so."

"That is so true, Bill. That's why I say the Katy's success is such a template for other communities to follow in order to help change their programs. I know that there are those who would say that you don't want to give the secrets away of being a champion. I was talking with Coach Johnston, and he told me that when his coaches were invited to speak to others about Katy's success that his coaches would ask him, 'What should we tell them about our program?' Coach would say, 'Tell them the truth. Listen, they are smart. They will watch the films and learn what we are doing. Never keep the right way to play the game from anyone.' I thought that this was a wonderful philosophy for Coach Johnston to have. On a larger scale, if communities, cities and countries are going to change their approach for winning, then it is important that we share what is working with others. If, in fact, what Katy has here can be a template for others to follow, then I hope that we can convey that ideal or concept in this book. Everyone wants to be a part of a winner. Yet, most people do not understand what it takes to be a champion. To me this community is the perfect template for that."

Bill added, "I was talking to our assistant athletic director. He used to be the Head Coach at Taylor High School. He admitted to me, of course, it was always a big rivalry when the two of us played. He said that the difference in Katy football is that these kids here go out on the football field expecting to win."

"To me, part of the success story of Katy football is the quality of the coaching, to build and teach the importance of having confidence to the kids...teaching not just the techniques of playing football but the teaching of having good character," agreed Floyd.

"It's interesting that you say that, Floyd, because one of the things that I notice is that most of the coaches whom I have interviewed who have truly made a difference have a foundation of Christ. They present it in their actions.

"While I research for *KatyNation*, I am finding that this is a great common denominator, a factor that seems to help put it all into layman's terms about the success Katy's football program. Whether the rest of the world can handle that or not remains to be seen. I, however, feel the presence of this common denominator with each contact that I make. What I see here is that it is really embedded into the foundation of this community. Just imagine having ten thousand communities like this."

Bill nodded in understanding. "One of the cute little stories that I failed to mention was one Dad told us about one of the football games down in Louise. He said that a tropical storm had come in, and it was raining like cats and dogs. He said that the field was pretty much under water. At one point, the umpire had to hold the football down with his foot just to keep it from floating away." We all laughed again. I didn't realize it at the time, but this interview was one that was filled with laughter and fun moments. "When you think of the quality of schools here in Katy, you have to understand that leadership is a key element. The big thing is that you have to have dedicated people, people who care about kids, especially teachers and coaches."

I asked Bill, "How do you find that? How has this community been so fortunate to have this element so abundantly?"

"Well, there are a couple of questions that come into play here. Is a good teacher or coach a natural, or are they trained? I think that it is a combination of both. You have to pick up on that when you are hiring them if they will be there for the kids day and night. I was so blessed to have lots of people like that."

"There is that word 'blessed' again, Bill. Throughout my research for this book, that word keeps popping up, 'blessed.' This leads me back to where the community's foundation lies. Another thing: everybody seems to be thankful for everybody else. This is something that you don't really see in this country today."

Floyd said, "Yes, like I said earlier, with so many churches in the beginning for such a small community, Christianity was that common thread that helped to keep everything together. There were lots of reasons why this community could have never gotten off the ground. I mean, these were the kids that went through the Depression like most of the country, and yet people here managed to find the strength and courage to see it through those challenging times.

"Our dad was in World War II in the Army Engineers. So many of these guys experienced war at such an early age. Jesse Bruton, one of my dad's teammates on that 1939 team, was in the Army Air Corps in Europe."

Bill said, "Wesley Buller was a tank commander in Europe and most of his division was wiped out in a battle."

"At my father's funeral, we put together this little piece about his life, and the thing that sort of jumped out at me the most was this: He had finished high school and spent several years in the Army fighting a war, but he was the father of four kids at age twenty-five, " continued Floyd.

"When I hear you talk about your dad being in the war, I am reminded of how little time that it has been since we have developed as a nation. Sitting here with you puts it into complete reality, knowing that your father lived in that time period. Both you and Floyd are a sort of a bridge that brings those times to the present. Just like your grandkids are the bridges to your past."

Bill answered, "Like I say, the football team is a sort of representative of the entire community. You will see people that you may never see any other time at a Katy Tiger football game. Some of the old graduates come back to see a Katy game."

"I understand what you mean. My first Katy game was last year over at Tulley stadium. I ran into my old quarterback Coach Eddie Otwell. Eddie coached me over at Eisenhower. I think that he said he was coaching over at Mayde Creek. The funny thing is that once you have a coach, he or she is always a coach to you. When I saw him, I shouted, 'Hey Coach!' Another thing about seeing a former coach is that when you see him, your relationship goes right back to where it left off. I remembered Eddie being up in my face after I had just thrown an interception. Today, especially as I research this book, I'm beginning to realize what a true blessing it is to be a coach. I'm sure, at the time, coaches don't realize the impact that they have on young kids' lives. These coaches contribute parts of themselves every single day. As a matter of fact, Coach Johnston was saying that it was not a job to him, that the first time he woke up and felt this was a job, he would be moving on. He said that you have to look forward to the opportunity to coach these kids.

"It is funny, guys, as a writer you can write from anywhere. I always saw my golden years up in the mountains somewhere living in a cabin, writing books. After being in Katy a while, I could actually see myself living in Katy. Lord knows that I never thought I would be saying that! I am sure, like a lot of people, I simply never thought of Katy having this kind of energy." We all laughed again. This was turning out to be a very helpful interview with the Haskett family. I knew that they had the true sense of this community and what it was all about.

"Bill, since you were here in 1981, you were a part of some very rough years. Tell me, how did you handle those rebuilding times? Coach Johnston mentioned that there was a time when he could have been forced to leave."

"Well, there were people that wanted Mike's head because we weren't winning. I had been out to practice and out to the field house enough to know that he was getting it started. I could see that Mike was putting a system in place. It was not just a matter of winning a game or two, but he was teaching Katy how to be winners down the road. It wasn't just about football.

"When I hired the band director, he was a Christian. I had seen what he had done in West Texas. I knew that our band program was not at 5A level. He asked me what I wanted him to do. I was very candid; I told him that I wanted him to produce a championship band.

"I knew, however, that it wasn't going to happen in the next year, that it was going to be a three, four-year project. In that time, I had to give him the support that he needed to get out there and get it done. He did; he made it happen. It's just a matter of hiring good people and giving them all the support that you can."

"Bill how do you keep the vultures off and away? You have the vision, because if you didn't you would not have hired them."

"In a sense it's a test of character. Most people want instant gratification. First, you have to have trust in your decisions that you make. Now that Mike has moved on, he left us with a system that is in place. Gary has taken the rings, and we are still winning. It will always be to Mike's credit that he put this system in place."

Floyd said, "Being on the outside looking in, I would think that it also said a lot about Bill's character through those struggling years. Instead of running Mike off and going out to get another, [he let him develop the team]."

"Right, you had to believe in what you were doing. Let's face it, Bill, when that adversity is there, that's where the test of character is presented. I always say that when we disagree with someone is when we find out how the other person stands. In that disagreement, if we maintain our respect for them, then we show our true character. To me, what you went through was a true example of leadership, Bill, and no doubt a role model of what role models should resemble. As we speak of role models, I had to laugh when I heard Charles Barkley say that he was no role model. How can any athlete on that level say that he is not a role model?"

Bill answered, "Yes he's a role model, maybe not a very good one. Like the dad that went out on the field and tackled a kid because his kid had been hit to hard by another player."

"Oh I saw that. That situation was a perfect example of what I was saying earlier. It's how you handle situations when you disagree that shows your true character. I understand that you can get caught up in the moment. I remember just the other night at Katy's homecoming game. I was on the sidelines when A&M Consolidated was about to score, and the player came around the end towards me, headed for the goal line. It took every thing that I had not to run out and tackle that kid. So you can find your self caught up in the moment." We all had a good laugh.

I never realized how time seemed to fly when I found myself interviewing someone about Katy's past. Each situation seemed to be so effortless and natural; it just flowed, and so did the time. I began to wrap up this particular interview. Bill said something that seemed to cap my purpose for being there.

"You know my daughter was in the drill team, and her director had an acronym for TEAM, Together Everyone Achieves Miracles."

I found that this statement to be one of those special "diamonds" that seemed to be found across the Katy community. Standing up, I thanked the Haskett sons for taking the time out of their day to share with me their thoughts about Katy High School football.

I felt that, though I didn't know Floyd Haskett Senior personally, I had a chance to meet him through the extension of his two sons. I left that meeting knowing that he was a hard-working man who believed in his community. I knew that he was not afraid to take on the responsibility of leadership. I knew this because it was still evident in his sons.

Even though Haskett was the quarterback of the first Katy School football team back in 1939, he was also the quarterback of some very special kids who obviously were not afraid to continue to carry the torch of leadership. Walking out of that office, I felt very strongly about what I was uncovering that made up the success of Katy's football program.

The powerful elements were also very simple. I could give my readers information that was, in reality, sitting right in front of them. Most people feel that there is some kind of magical philosophy behind the success of winning. What is behind Katy's success story is something that we all have at our disposal: persistence, discipline, and leadership. Whether are not this nation chooses to believe and apply it, only time will tell.

Planting the Good Seeds

Coach Gordon Brown

Most people would not understand it if you told them that building a football program was a lot like planting seeds, that you must prepare the "soil" and those around it for change and for a good successful harvest. They might not understand, when I say that you might have to make some changes and do things a little differently than what was done years before. In a way it is kind of ironic that the community of early Katy was comprised mostly of farmers...seed planters who worked the soil, doing whatever it took along the way to produce a successful harvest...creating a successful football program for Katy. Powerful seeds were exactly the things that I uncovered to be a part of the Katy football program.

It was a couple of weeks past Richard Fussell's wake. I am not really sure why I waited to contact Coach Gordon Brown. My brief meeting with him told me that he was a special man, easy to communicate with and possessing both a delightful spirit and a very positive energy. His wife Genevieve seemed more excited about the book *KatyNation* than he did. Of course, considering we met at a wake, I could understand. I guess in some way I wanted to continue letting this book happen naturally.

Therefore, I didn't rush into a meeting with Coach. It

was a Thursday afternoon when I made my first contact with him. After I left a message with his service, he returned my call with the hour. I remember feeling like a kid on the phone. Even as an adult, there is something about coaches which seemed to invoke a spirit of appreciation and ultimate respect from me. Maybe it was because I never knew my father in my childhood that all my coaches through the years seemed to step into that role for me. All I can really say about it is that I will always keep a special place in my heart for the role of the coach.

My phone conversation with Coach Brown was more like a former player having a chance to talk with one of his former coaches. Hearing the excitement about my project in his voice helped to fuel the acknowledgment that I was on the right path. It reassured me that the passion I knew existed in Katy Tiger football was not there by accident. Coach Brown's excitement about the book was just what I needed to become even more dedicated and committed to this project.

I originally thought that he wasn't that interested, but he was truly excited about the book that I was writing, even though he didn't show it a the wake. He seemed to welcome our meeting. He and his wife were having a dinner party for a number of coaches that weekend. So we scheduled our interview the following Tuesday, around 1:00 p.m.

When I got off the phone with him, I was simply beside myself. I was meeting with the coach who planted the first seeds that helped to make the Katy Tiger football team what it is today. The only thing that I could compare my excitement to was the time that I got off the phone with King Hill, the wide receiver coach of the Houston Oilers. After him telling me that the Oilers were going to sign me to a two-year contract, Coach Hill asked me if I could find the time to meet with him to sign the contract. I couldn't believe what I was hearing! Could I find the time? I would have propelled myself from a cannon to get over to Fannin Street back then! When Coach Brown asked me if I could make it on Tuesday, I was overwhelmed with joy. "Hey are you going to bring your clubs?" he asked.

"Yes, sure," I replied. I didn't realize that he had heard me tell Genevieve at the wake that I played a little golf. Coach gave me directions to their home, and the opening kickoff was about to happen.

Tuesday morning, I was on the road about 10:00 a.m. For some reason, I remembered Huntsville to be a lot further away than it seemed on this trip. Like Katy to the west of Houston, Huntsville, to the north, had extended itself as only a stone's throw away from the great metropolitan city. I was impressed by the growth which had been created in my twenty-year absence from the Houston area. The freeway was now lined with new life and lots of signs of growth. Home Depots and Wal*Marts dotted the frontage roads that once were acres and acres of wooded forest. Gated communities and shopping malls plentifully adorned I-45.

I arrived in Elkin's Lake literally an hour and a half before my meeting with Coach. I remember back when general conversation was centered on the building of the exclusive community called Elkin's Lake. It was to be a big, exclusive area just north of Conroe, featuring homes surrounding a beautiful man-made lake. Yet this was my first time to see it for myself. Coach's directions were perfect.

I found myself sitting in my truck watching the local activity around the golf course, not wanting to be too early. My initial thoughts as I sat there were of how I could take something from this meeting, which would help the community of Katy to better appreciate its football heritage. I wanted to be able to give the citizens a little background knowledge about the road to their present-day success. I started to feel a little pressured.

I knew that Katy was a proud community. How could I help inspire them in regards to their football heritage? I knew that this was not going to be an easy task. The energy and excitement of this community was already second to none.

I knew that this was a football community that had put great demands on itself. I remembered when I put up my first website to give the community of Katy an opportunity to learn more about the book that an outsider was writing. Well, let's just say that if you come into Katy, you better not come in half-stepping, as the saying goes. I watched the Booster Club website the following week after the news was released. I got a crash course of how passionate the community was about their Tigers. I realized then and there that I had better do my homework if I was going to do this community any justice at all. I was going to have to find information that they did not know about themselves. I knew that the verdict was still out about my efforts and me, so I chose to look at the glass being half full rather than half empty.

I remember one episode where a gentleman from Katy about the *KatyNation* website contacted me. He introduced himself and was both direct and to the point. His suggestion was that if I was serious about writing a book about Katy High School football, then I really needed a much better website if I wanted to present myself to the community.

I have never been married before, but I would equate it to having a wife stop her husband at the front door and say, "Honey, you are not wearing that shirt out in public, are you?" and present him with a much better alternative. Well, I have learned that in order to continue growing in life that it is important to find a way to digest criticism so that it is not bitter or distasteful. So, I managed to put aside my ego and welcome Roberts Willeby's suggestions.

When I did that, what I saw in him was a genuine concern to continue to carry the touch of excellence of Katy's football community. Two days later, Robert presented me with the new and improved website for *KatyNation*. Without asking for one single dime, he took the material and made it presentable. Viewing the new website for the first time made my heart skip a beat. It was truly the most professional presentation that I had seen, even in my twenty years around production companies in Los Angeles. Two and a half years on the *Star Trek: the Next Generation* television series gave me an idea what real professionals have the power to do.

In many ways, it is hard to digest that your best is not good enough, but when you see something better, it also helps to increase your understanding that we can always do more. Being better is simply a work in progress. Robert Willeby did more for me in his kind gesture than I had learned in many years of life. He helped me realize that the responsibility that I was taking on was far greater than I could imagine. If I stayed on the right path, God would grant me with the necessary gifts along the way that would see me through this project. I still have never met Robert Willeby, but every time I send a person to the *KatyNation* website, I smile, knowing that he was one of the many gifts I have received along the way as I'm writing this book. I promised myself that I would someday pass a blessing like this on to someone else. Hopefully that blessing will be passed on, and through the power of the seed that Robert planted, many others will find support along their journeys. I have found countless seed planters living in Katy Texas. They are real, and they are living among you.

Suddenly, I heard a shout, some one crying out

"Fore!" which broke my train of thought. I looked up to see a golf ball jumping over a few yards near the parking lot. Apparently someone else had been to the Dexter Clay School of Golf.

I smiled to myself, for I surely knew that feeling of having a golf ball get away from you. Even though I was still forty-five minutes early, I decided that going in to the coach's office might not be a bad Idea. Okay, so it could have been the 98-degree temperature that also helped me make that decision.

I introduced myself to his secretary and told her that I was a little early and that I was going upstairs to have a bite to eat. After ordering a slice beef sandwich with a giant lemonade, I found myself staring out over the fairway which lined the back of the restaurant. There were two women at a couple of tables away from me chatting away. About ten minutes later, one lady got up to go, leaving the other lady and I staring at each other only two tables apart. I'm not just sure who started the conversation, but after awhile, we were talking up a breeze.

I told her that I had a meeting with Gordon Brown. When I mentioned that, her eyes lit up. "Gordon is a lifesaver," she said, "for us here in the community." She went on to explain that Coach Brown had stepped in as the Interim Director and had changed a negative situation into a positive one for those in the association there. She told me that years back, Coach had held the position, but when he retired, everything "went south," as they say. They then talked him into coming back for a few more years, and a couple of years after he had left for the last time, they asked him if he would take the office in the interim while they found someone who was qualified.

Coach agreed under the terms that he would not

accept a salary. He was volunteering his time to help the organization get back on his feet. This lady continued to praise Coach's efforts, not knowing why I was there. Soon her husband arrived, and he sat down, and to my amazement, continued to carry the torch of Coach's priceless value to the community. They asked me if I lived in the community. I said that I did not, that I was there to interview Coach for a book that I was working on.

"Oh, I did not know that Gordon was a coach, did you hon?"

"I think that I heard that Gordon was a coach somewhere." Right on cue, Coach came around the corner into the restaurant. It was nice to see him again. I noted that energy in the whole restaurant changed when he entered. As the waiter brought my check, Coach grabbed and signed it, and we were off towards his office.

Even though Gordon was no longer coaching, being in a coach's office always brought back some kind of memories for me. He had to make a couple of phone calls first, and then we could begin our interview. Looking around the rather large office, I saw no visible signs that Coach Brown ever coached a day of football in his life. The office was adorned with maps of the community and other items reflecting development of the Elkin's Lake area.

Coach Brown was finally freed from his responsibilities, and we began to talk a little. First, we talked about what I would like to accomplish with the *KatyNation* project. The coach suggested a game plan for the day. I was excited to learn that I was going to be spending the whole day with him, and not just a few minutes. I started to feel like a kid in a candy store. There was something very special about Katy football coaches. I hadn't put my finger on it yet, but I made myself a promise that if I could narrow this element, that I would be able to figure out at least part of their success formula.

Since I had the whole day with Coach Brown, it was not like having to record everything right away. We spent about twenty minutes in his office, and then he said, "Let me take you around Huntsville a little and show you some of the things that we are doing here."

Coach Brown and I got in his car, and off we went for a tour. Our first stop was the Elkin's Lake community. I could hear his pride for his community in his voice. He might not have been taking a salary, but you would have never known it by his passion for the area. He showed me the streets that were being repaired. He told me their challenges with silt in the lakes. He had figured out a way out to extract it from the three lakes.

If I didn't know any better, I might have thought Coach Brown had built those lakes himself. He slowed down to wave at the guy on the bulldozer, calling him by his name. If in fact, love for one's community were ever to be measured by mankind, Ex-Head Football Coach of the Katy Tigers Gordon Brown would be found in The Love for Community Hall of Fame. The sincerity of his conversation was real and rewarding. Have you ever been around someone who makes you feel like you want to be a better person? This is the kind of person who brought the first state championship to Katy Texas.

As we pulled out to I-45 into the city of Huntsville, Coach pointed out this and that about different activities going on in the neighborhood. Coach was proud of his community, but I would soon find out that he was even more excited about Sam Houston State University. It was more than the fact that his wife Genevieve was Dean of Education there. He had his hand on the pulse of the University's growth and, because of that, he was excited. He spoke of the great job a new dean was doing there. It did not dawn on me at that time, but everything that came out of Coach's mouth was of a positive nature. If, in fact, there was such a thing as the power of positive thoughts, I was about to be a by-product of association

Obviously, one of Katy's secret weapons was its former head coach. To listen to Coach Brown speak was invigorating. Suddenly, the thought hit me that I was driving through Sam Houston State University, being given a personal tour by one of Katy's High School's legendary coaches. Whoever said research had to be boring never lived in Katy, Texas. I was having the time of my life, and this was only the first hour of our visit.

"Oh, you have got to see this." Coach said as he turned down a narrow, rustic road. Apparently, Sam Houston actually did some of his writing in one of the small buildings which sat on the side of this particular road. Then Coach Brown made a turn in a small driveway and stopped about a hundred feet away in a clear opening between two buildings.

"You see that field? I played football on that field."

"Wow, Coach that's amazing!"

"The field is still being used today by Sam Houston's soccer team. Prichet Field it was called." Seeing that old field must have brought back great memories for Coach. He had the look of a kid in his eyes. Then he shared a story with me that I will never forget.

He pointed at the corner of the field, and said, "You see over there at the south end of the field? Well, when it rained, the water would back up into the end zone, to about the ten-yard line. Well I was quarter backing a game when I was hit so hard, that even to this day, I remember the lick. The guy smothered my face in this huge puddle of water setting on that end of the field. Well, guess who that guy was?" Silence pervaded our vehicle. I could not even begin to imagine. "Do you remember the old television show *Bonanza*?"

"Yes, I do," I replied.

"Well I took that wallop from Hoss Cartwright. Dan Blocker."

"Wow!" This time instead of feeling like a little boy, I became one! "You're kidding me, Coach; you got hit by Hoss Cartwright?" I could hear that theme song playing in my head. DOOM Diee Doom Diee Doom Doom. "Wow! I used to watch that show all the time!"

This little story captured my imagination to the point that I totally forgot why I was there. I was having such a great time that it didn't dawn on me that I should be recording this. Coach drove off, and we both had smiles on our faces as if we had been hanging out together for years. We drove on past the new baseball stadium and continued to tour the campus. He showed me where Genevieve's office was located. The university had change considerably over the years.

As we moved out toward the interstate, Coach showed me where the public golf course was, and then he suggested that we go back to his home so he could change and get his clubs. Then reality jumped to the forefront. I'm not a good golfer. Oh well, if Coach was truly a patient man, he was about to be tested in the next half hour.

Coach's home was a reflection of himself. Quiet and peaceful, it sat upon a grassy hill. A half-circle driveway presented itself out front, and there a side driveway which took you to the back garage. When I got out of my truck to walk towards the back, I realized that I was in serious trouble. There it was, sitting there like a large predator. I tried not to be intimidated when I walked through the garage. But as I viewed Coach's weapons of choice I knew that I was about to be destroyed. There was the golf cart of Coach Gordon Brown. A man with his own golf cart is like a pro golfer from where I come from. I walked proudly past the cart, not to let it see my knees about to buckle, while I shouted at the door, "Hey, Coach, I'm here."

Coach was already inside. "There is some water and a banana on the kitchen counter if you like," he said as he walked down the hallway towards the back of the house. Inside, the house was something from *House and Garden* magazine. It was almost difficult to tell that anyone actually lived there. It seemed like everything was in order. I looked around to find clues but could not. "I'll be right out, so make yourself at home," Coach shouted from a back room.

About five minutes later, Coach Brown came out in his golf attire with big smile of his face.

Before we left, Coach gave me a brief tour of the house. He was so comfortable with the task that I think Coach must have been a tour guide in another lifetime. He was very thorough in his presentation about the application of their unique floors to the stories behind the grandkids' pictures that covered the entire refrigerator.

Then we reached his office. He mentioned that he wanted to have the office redone but had not gotten to it yet. I thought it was perfect. Suddenly, I saw The Wall. I walked over to it on the right side of his office. It had the feel of a football altar adorned with old footballs, trophies, plaques, and pictures. I had hit the mother load. For a few moments, there was complete silence between us. Coach just stood there with a smile on his face. He knew that he was about to present me with the reason that I had come to see him.

"Coach, this is amazing," I believe were my first words. It was here that I felt the essence of Katy Tiger history. I knelt down so that I could really appreciate the two large brown leather-bound scrapbooks that Coach had sitting on the top of the bookcase. As he opened to the first page, I wished every Katy fan could be with me at that very moment. I'm not sure why it is, but the best moments in our lives often happen when no one else is around to share it with us. The first page was filled with old Katy High School ribbons. They were very well preserved, considering that they were well over forty-seven years old..."Go Katy" and "Katy #1." There was even one that had "Go Katy Tigers" on it.

Then Coach began his presentation.

"The funny thing about those ribbons back then was that if you did not wear one in school, you were considered a person who did not support the team. So 95% of the school wore the ribbons during football season." Next to the ribbons, there was a picture of the old stands. My mind raced back to the first time that I set foot on the Tigers' field. I remembered the section of stands still there today. I thought it odd that the there was a complete new section of stands, and there on the end, sat this rustic section of bleachers.

"This kid here was is Stanley MacDonald. He was the valedictorian of his class. He is no longer living now. He went on to play football at Rice University and later married. One morning he climbed into the attic to fix the AC and was electrocuted. Most people didn't know it, but Stanley's father was our custodian at Katy. Before that, he worked at a number of farms in the area. As a matter of fact, when I first got to Katy, the football field was like playing on concrete. A couple of school board members volunteered their equipment to rework the field. Stanley's dad drove the tractor and suggested that we mix some old rotten rice hulls into the dirt. This made it much softer. We had the one of the softest football fields in our district for years to come."

I then came across a picture of Farriel Culpepper.
"Oh, so this is Culpepper. I hear this kid was a real work
horse, Coach."
    He replied with a very satisfied smile on his face.
"Yes, he was the real deal! He went on to play at TCU. My
favorite Culpepper story was... you know coaches remember
the unusual things that happen with their boys? A few years
after winning state that year, one of the ex-players that played
for Berni High School, which we played in Seguin in the
quarterfinals, came to Katy as assistant athletic director. Well,
he reminded me of just how tough that Culpepper was. He
said to me, 'Coach, I remember playing you guys up in
Seguin for the quarterfinals in the playoffs. Well, do you
remember the time that the ambulance came out onto the
field? Well, I had been begging my coach the whole game to
let me in so that I could put a licking on that Culpepper kid.
"Come on Coach he doesn't look that tough." Well, by the
fourth quarter, Coach finally let me into the game. On the
first play, I found myself standing in the direct line of path of
Culpepper carrying the ball. Well, all I remember was being
hit by him, and then I remember being put into that
ambulance. That was me in that ambulance, Coach.'"
    Coach Brown had different smiles when he told
different stories. This one, was that of a proud father. Then I
came across this old paper flier. It said, "Attention All
Mothers! Any mother willing to help feed the boys for three
days, please call Coach Brown."
    "This was around the time of the beginning of football
season. I wanted to keep the boys at practice during two-a-
days so that I could keep an eye on them. Getting the mothers
involved was a great thing. They began to get a better
understanding of how the game was played and soon became
excited about the team. The mothers' excitement passed on to

the fathers, and soon everyone became a part of the program."

"Coach, in a way, you didn't know it at the time, but you helped to plant the first seed for the awesome Booster Club that Katy has today."

"Well, I never thought about it, but I guess maybe you could say that I did have something to do with that.

"You know when I first came to Katy, Jack Rhodes was the Principal then. Well, by my third day on the job, three of the junior players came to me: Jack Roades [a student and a later coach], Albert Thomson and John Culpepper. 'Coach,' they said, 'we heard that you were here, and we wanted to stop by to meet you. We also wanted to let you know that we want to win, Coach! We will do what it takes, but we want to win!' I give those young men the credit for planting the seeds of Katy High School football. I could see it in their eyes. They were not just talking; they came with a commitment to play the game.

"One of my biggest challenges back then was to get the players believing that they could win, then transferring that belief to the families. Most of the people were related; most them went to school there and stayed and worked the farms. So there was this incredible bond that was there. When I first arrived at Katy, the whole football program was basically housed in a ten-foot by ten-foot storage room. I will never forget looking up at the old leather helmets as they sat up on top of old tomato cans. We had to wear those old helmets the first couple of seasons before the program could afford to get new ones."

"So, Coach, you mean while the other schools had newer model helmets, Katy had to wear the old leather/plastic ones?"

"Yes, that's right, we sure did."

As if right on cue, I came across an old article from

1956. It was entitled "The History of Katy Football." I read it out loud. "'Football started in Katy in the fall of 1939. Ned Reader was the head coach, assistant coach and the trainer.'"

Coach interrupted, smiling as he said, "they sure got their money's worth back then."

Continuing, I read, "'Through the efforts of the Dad's Club, enough private donations were gathered to equip about twelve players. R. E. McClory donated the first football to the program. Each kid had to furnish his own shoes. Approximately twenty-five kids showed up for the first workout. After a couple of sessions of blocking and tackling, about half of the kids decided against the game. Coach Reader selected six men. Back then, fans walked the sidelines because there were no stands for them to sit. Katy lost its first game by the scoring rule, which prevented the contest from going on after their opponent scored fifty points or more.' Wow, Coach, those were some very humble beginnings," I said.

"Yes they were. When I came to Katy, I was the Athletic Director, Head Football Coach, Head Basketball Coach, Head Track Coach, and the Director of Summer Recreations.

"Most of our conditioning back then was made up of drills. We did not have weights then, so we took those old gallon tomato cans and filled them with cement and placed steel rods into them, creating bar bells and worked out with that to help build our strength. The big thing in those days was trying to teach the kids that they could win. It started with me. I had a thing back in that day that I would not come into practice on Mondays unless that I was convinced that we could win.

"This was a pretty challenging thing to do at times, especially our big game against Sundown. I knew that we were about to play a pretty powerful team. They had an explosive offense, averaging well over forty-five points per game. The superintendent and I took a small plane to scout out Sundance's Semifinal game. Their quarterback went on to play for Rice University. They had a running back that was All Star as a sophomore. So I knew that we had our work cut out for us...I saw that they were strong and fast.

" By Monday practice time, I had convinced myself that we could beat them. I never dreamed, however, that our defense would hold them to only six points. That's Charles Peck, remarkable kid he was. He never played football until his junior year. He used to come to watch his older brother practice every day. I remember as if it were yesterday. I walked over to the Cyclone fence one day while practice was going, and said to Charlie. 'You know, one day I'm going to get you on this side of the fence.' He looked at me and said, 'Who? Me?' 'Yes, you,' I said. I have never seen a kid come along faster in all my days coaching. He was about 6'3" and could move. He started for us his senior year at Katy. He went only to junior college and became an All American.

"You have to recruit when you have a small program like we had back then. One player could make the difference in whether or not you had a good season or a great one. Charlie was one of those players that only come around every once in awhile. Know that Charlie Shafer? You mentioned that you spoke to him."

"Yes I did. Charlie was one of the first players that I interviewed."

"Well, Charlie was fun to watch. He would simply glide across the football field. It was Charlie Shafer's kick return that won the game for us back in 1959. I remember that he fumbled the ball momentarily, and when he picked up the ball, there were three of Sundance's players around him.

"Somehow, he made them all miss him, and off it went! That was sure nice to watch." Pointing at another player, Gordon said, "This was Albert Voight, a fine player. He had an irregular heartbeat. The doctor suggested that he be rested periodically. So, we played him mostly on offense. Occasionally, we would rest him up for defenses when we needed a goal line stance or something like that. Oh, these were the schools in our district back then." He read them aloud, "Eagle Lake, Hitchcock, Pearland, Dulles, East Bernard and Sealy."

"Coach, did you feel at the beginning of the season that you would have that kind of a year?"

"Well, I felt that if we stayed healthy that would be all right. Of course we lost Jerry Goynes at the end to a broken leg in the Hitchcock game. I knew that the team was going to be special because five of the kids played together in junior high school."

There were many great articles collected in Coach's book. "Lots of great articles here, Coach," I said.

"Yes, you know how we got such great coverage back then? Well, there were two sisters that did the sports section for the *Brookshire Times* back then. Well they were very nice ladies, but they didn't know a whole lot about football. So, I found that it was simpler for me to just write the article and turn them into them. It really helped to keep us in the paper back then."

"Coach, was there anything more about the state game that you remember?"

"Oh yes, how a little scouting trip turned out to be to our advantage. Sundance had this three running back set. We had encountered it earlier in the year against Sugarland. Well, after watching them for a while, I realized that 99% of the time, their blocking back would 'telegraph' where their plays were going. So, I made an adjustment with our defense. I placed seven men up front, putting our two best linebackers in the middle. Well, beating Sugarland gave the boys the conviction needed to win. By the time we got to state, they believed that they could win. Most of the papers had us as the underdogs, though. That game was played in Brownwood. By the time that we got there, the other team was already there. Well, as we got off the bus, someone from the other team threw some ice down from one of the windows. I heard Dwayne Fussell say, 'Wait until we get them on the field; we will cool them off.' I realized then the kids were ready to play."

Coach finally walked over to sit down behind his desk. "You know I was in awe of how the community came together to support us. The sheriff said that there were fewer than eleven people left in the city when we went to Brownwood. Maybe he was exaggerating a bit, but not a whole lot. There is something about winning that changes things for people. It is as if their belief starts to come to life. I know that the people in Katy started to believe."

I started to think about the verse in Matthew. "If ye have Faith as a grain of mustard seed, ye shall say unto this mountain, Remove hence to yonder place and it shall move; and nothing shall be impossible unto you." However, I pondered where the belief actually gets started in a person or in a community. I am sure that in all the early years of Katy's football history, there had to be countless who believed. I wondered at what point in faith did belief manifest itself into reality.

One thing is for sure: winning has the remarkable ability to bring people together. Its power flows far beyond personal attitudes and philosophies into a realm of acceptance like none other. Its energies cross race barriers and political differences. I had always heard that we must somehow learn to enjoy the ride along the way in life. Sitting in that small office with Coach made that saying become a reality. Another small spark of understanding to the success of Katy Tiger football was at hand.

Coach Brown's first look at Katy's locker room 1954.

1959 State Championship Team.

1959 Tiger team. Top Row: Gordon Brown (Head Coach), Warren
Walding, Lynn Sturm, Stanley McDonald, Charles Peck, Roy
Wiesner, Jerry Goynes, Alfred Peck, Lenny Steffens, Volan

Youngblood, Fred Hluchen (Jr. High Coach). Middle Row: Joe
Bright (Line Coach). Doug Gilbert, Tommy Wolters, Joe Carroll,
Ross Spencer, Richard Fussell, Thad Smith, Albert Voight, Paul
Short, Vincent Perez, Fred Ruland (Jr. High Coach). Lower Row:
Jim Bone (Trainer), Bill Madsen, Butch Polan, Bill Jordan, Dwayne
Fussell (Captian.), Farriel Cilpepper (Capt.), Charlie Shafer, Larry
Newman, James Griffin, Ralph Myers, Bill Bone (Mgr.). Front: Ray
Mangum (Mgr.).

The teams that are taking the football field today are
simply the manifestation of seeds planted long before their
time by "farmers" who helped to nurture their football
programs with hard work and discipline. They were humble
servants who were not afraid to ask God to bless their efforts.
Coach and I talked for a couple of hours in his office. I

suddenly realized that we both had started to feel drained from the talk. Right about that time, Coach looked down at his watch. "Well, we better head over to the course before it gets too late. It was amazing; it was like a new energy had come into the room. Golf is truly an amazing game. All of a sudden, we both started to act like two high school boys.

We hopped in Coach's cart and headed down the road. The course was only about a half a mile away from his home. It seemed like everyone that we passed by waved at Coach along the way. I felt like the only thing that was missing was the Secret Service team. I don't know why it came to a surprise to me, but Coach Brown was as gracious on the golf course as he had been all afternoon.

It was just the two of us hitting the ball late into the afternoon. I must be honest; he did most of the hitting. I, for some reason, spent a lot of time looking in the trees for my ball. But Coach was encouraging and always seemed to have a great attitude. We rode along until about the 16th hole, when we got a call from his Other Half, and we took off to clean up for dinner.

It was at the restaurant that evening that I fully understood the power behind Coach Gordon Brown's personality. After the appetizers arrived, Coach offered to bless the foods. It was in that blessing that I heard the voice of his passion for life. In that voice, I heard the humble spirit which recognized that every increase that comes to man comes through God first. I knew that I was not dining with ordinary people. The Brown's had been anointed, and it showed in every aspect of their lives.

I was sitting at the table with one Katy's early seed planters. The harvest of success that we see today with the Katy Tigers had been enriched in the soil of this heritage.

My drive back to Houston that night seemed only five to

ten minutes long. When Coach and Genevieve both gave me hugs at the front door, I felt as if I were leaving family members. I looked back when I turned out of driveway. Coach had one arm around his wife and the other hand was waving goodbye to me.

If this were, in fact, the kind of seeds that had been planted in the early stages of Katy's program, there was no doubt why its success continued.

Coach Brown and I, to this day, talk once every two weeks on the phone. I knew that I had gained more than just a subject to interview for my book. I had also found myself befriended by of the greatest figures in the history of Katy football. One thing that I became strongly aware of was that, early in its foundation, Katy had managed to hire men of faith and great character, coaches who lay their hands upon the helmets of kids, nurturing them along the way to become champions.

It was about six weeks later before I saw Coach Brown again. He called me to let me know that the *Houston Chronicle* was doing a story on the Katy Tigers of 1959 and needed to shoot some pictures.

Coach Brown suggested that I come along. I was really appreciative of the fact that Coach considered me to be a part of Katy football now. The photo shoot was held on a Friday at 5:00 p.m., over at Rhodes Stadium Field House in Katy.

I walked around into the open gate which led to the back of the field house. The stadium was completely empty, except for a couple of maintenance attendants washing down the stands. It was a hot Texas afternoon, and I thought that those guys had the right idea by hosing down everything.

I passed one of the big picture windows which separated the door to the back entry. I could see that five or six people were already inside. Walking inside, I saw Coach Brown standing in the hallway talking to a young lady. I smiled, walking slowly in their direction. Giving him a hug, I said that it was good to see him.

Coach then introduced me to Debbie Decker. Debbie was one of Katy's Assistant Directors of Athletics. She seemed to be very warm and made sure that everything was running smoothly. I think that it was after meeting Debbie that I realize that KISD recruited personable individuals who really enjoyed what they were doing. Could this also be a factor in the overall progress of its successful winning ways?

Coach Brown then took me into the room and introduced me to the people inside. Tom Behrens, a freelance writer shooting pictures for the *Chronicle* was the first person that I met. As Coach went around the room, I realized that the men in the room were a strong part of Coach's past. Each man that Coach Brown introduced to me as I shook his hand was a player from the 1959 team.

It was at this time that I felt that history had taken its long arm and found a way to embrace the present. There were only four players and one player's wife in the room. Each player held an old Katy football jersey in his hand. My mind quickly took me back to when I first looked upon the picture of the Katy Tiger squad of 1959 at Brookshire Brothers. A few of the players had jumped off of the large portrait and found their way into the present.

Larry Newman, #22; Ralph Myers, #41; Albert Voight, #64; and Thad Smith, #52 were all standing before me. Then Coach said, "Dexter, tell them what you are doing." When you are doing a project of this nature, you never know when you will be asked to present it to others. This time my presentation was to those individuals who were directly involved, men who lived the story that I was writing.

125

"To make a long story short, I am writing a book about the history of the Katy Tiger football program. I will then write a screenplay in hopes that the book creates enough interest to become a movie someday. The history of Katy football is such a wonderful story that I honestly believe that it has the potential to become a feature film." I told them that I had been in Hollywood for the last twenty years and that I had been a part of the industry long enough to see that this story was good enough to be on the big screen.

As the silence settled in the room from my conversation, I could see the faces of these guys hanging their smiles on every word that I spoke. I began to feel a little like a writer pitching a story to a room filled with producers; only these producers had lived the story countless years before me.

By six o'clock, only four players and Coach Brown had gathered at the field house. Tom, the *Chronicle's* photographer, decided to photograph those present. The players were asked to put their jerseys on. Well, all the players had the same challenge with their jersey. Let's just say that time had found a way to shrink those jerseys. Albert and Larry managed to force their way into theirs. Soon, Ralph followed. Thad's jersey, however, was not going to be bullied by his efforts, so he ended up simply placing it over his shoulder. In all fairness, the jerseys were a little small in the first place.

The five warriors of Katy's past moved outside towards the goal post on the north side of Rhodes Stadium. I think that Coach Brown was a little disappointed that more of the guys didn't find away to make it, but he never showed it. I simply had a feeling that he was. I had Charlie Shafer's office number with me and tried to contact him, but to no avail.

Debbie and I walked together out on the field about ten yards behind the members of the 1959 squad. They were now only five. At least for this picture their numbers had dwindled to that amount. Before the photographer took the shot, I suggested that he place Coach in the middle and have two players on each side of him. I am not sure why; it just seemed to made more sense than for Coach Brown to be on the end.

After about six or seven pictures, I asked Tom if he would get a shot of Coach and me together. As Coach Brown and I stood side by side, each sharing an end of the actual game ball from the 1959 championship team, I realized that I had come a long way from the conception of the book.

It had become increasingly clear that the power of human thoughts was very real. One single thought had manifested itself into reality.

There I was, standing next to the coach who had planted the first, most powerful seed of success in Katy's history. I could not have been more proud. As we stood there, the 100-yard field as our backdrop, I considered this as a gift presented directly to me from the universe.

Walking back towards the field house, I could hear Coach Brown sharing stories with the four players who were present. I sort of backed away a little because I have learned that some of my best material comes from watching from a distance. It was certainly true in this case. I found myself capturing a moment in time, recording the uniqueness of the past meeting the present.

This was something incredible to watch. I was given a window which allowed me to see history and the present simultaneously. Looking at Coach Brown sharing old stories with his players, I could honestly envision the players as kids back in high school. From the way they smiled and laughed, telling jokes about the past, I could see the boyish faces in the men who were standing before me. It was then that I thought to myself, maybe this was what was so great about Katy's football history, that somehow, its history had found a way to exist in the present as well.

Suddenly, one player's cell phone went off, breaking up the window of timelessness. While we stood in the back of the field house listening to the conversation, we all learned at the same time that one of the other players, Joe Carroll, # 61 in your program, had been driving around at another location with Charlie Shafer.

Joe was given the instructions by his old teammate Larry Newman. When Larry got off the phone, he said that Joe was ten minutes away. I then asked Tom if he didn't mind waiting another ten minutes so that we could include one more player into the photos. Tom graciously agreed, and soon Joe showed up. I watched as his team welcomed him into the group like a missing cub finding his family after being lost for a while. Debbie and I watched from a distance as the small gathering repeated its photos session.

As each of the players reluctantly said his goodbyes, I knew that I had been a part of something super special at Rhodes Stadium that evening. Coach Brown and I were the last two remaining in the parking lot surrounded by empty spaces. He went to his SUV and presented me with a copy of a picture of old leather football helmets that his daughter had gathered together for us. I told Coach weeks before that I was considering using a picture of an old leather helmet as the cover of the book. So, he offered to look around to see if he had something that might be suitable.

I thanked Coach Brown for inviting me out to join this evening. I will never forget his words, "I had some really good kids back then. I have been blessed to be a part of something very special here at Katy." Then he said to me, "What you are doing is a really good thing, you know!"

I smiled and replied, "Thank you, Coach." I told him that it was I who felt blessed. It was the second time I had been reminded by a member of Katy's past, about how special this project was. The first was after my first telephone conversation with Harold Andrews who totally blew me away when he said, "Thank you for writing this book. This is a book whose time is way overdue."

I sat in my truck and watched as Coach Brown's SUV drove towards the gate that evening. I didn't want to drive away. That evening had offered me another precious moment, and I wanted to appreciate every single bit of it.

A Tiger on the Line

Coach Joe Bright

There is doubt that times have changed quiet dramatically when it comes to coaching the game of football. One of the most apparent changes can be found in the number of coaches that a team has in its program. Though each team can be divided in offense and defense, each of those two elements can be broken down into four or five different specialty coaches.

That was not the case back in 1959 when Katy football won its first State Championship title. Coach Gordon Brown had only one ally who accompanied him as he marched into battle; his name was Joe Bright. I first saw Coach Joe Bright in a newspaper clipping that Dough Gilbert, who played on that '59 team, gave me. Doug had also given me an old roster with telephone numbers on it. Most of the numbers had been changed. I tried the number next to Coach Bright's name.

Though the area code had changed, the number was the same. Coach Bright's wife Jeannie answered the phone, and I shared with her my purpose for the call. Jeannine was a pleasant lady who sounded very excited to find out that I was writing a book on Katy's football history. She assured me that she would pass the information along to her husband once he got in.

The story of the Katy Tigers' history was a puzzle with its pieces scattered throughout the community. I had wondered why no one had taken the time to gather them all and place them for everyone to see. Then I realized who that someone was, and that someone just happened to be me. Each contact that I made seemed to help me continue creating a beautiful portrait.

A couple of days later, I spoke to Coach Bright on the phone. He like, everyone else that I made contact with, was excited about someone writing a book about Katy's football history. A couple of weeks later I met up with Coach Bright at another Katy High School named Mayde Creek. The day arrived when I found myself on the campus of Mayde Creek High School.

Not knowing exactly about where I was going, I found myself walking around the campus searching for Coach Bright's location. I stopped to ask two students if they had heard of Coach Bright. They answered "No Sir" simultaneously. It's a strange thing to hear a child call you "Sir." It is such a respectful gesture, which at the same time reminds you that you will never be a kid again. One of them suggested that I try the front office. I told them "Thanks," and headed through the school towards the front.

Apparently Mayde Creek offers an adult program, and Coach Bright worked the front desk part time. Passing a couple of ladies cleaning the floors, I said 'Excuse me," as I walked into the front office. Walking by the glass front to the administration office, I could see Coach Bright staring into a computer's monitor. Dressed in a pair of overalls, he looked like he had stepped out of the past. With his crew cut hairstyle, I recognized him right away from the old picture that I had seen of him.

Coach's jolly energy made be feel extremely welcome when I introduced myself. I was anxious to hear his words about early Katy. Again, I was about to be rewarded with the gift to walk back in time. This was becoming something that I enjoyed the most about the researching Katy High School football. And those two youngsters had just reminded me that the past was something that we all can look forward to joining. Yes, sir, that is the truth, like it or not.

Coach Bright didn't waste anytime asking me questions. "Well how much do you know about Katy's school district?" I said that everything that I had learned had been in about the last six months. It was then that I shared with him about how this whole book came about. I explained to him how I was finding that there was a great deal of information about Katy's history and that others had told me that I should maintain my focus. This was my main reason for deciding to write about Katy High School football in two books, instead of just one.

I told him that this book was more of a nostalgic piece. I told him that I wanted the kids who are a part of Katy's successful program today to understand the origins of their heritage.

"Now, did you come into the understanding that Katy's school district was not always down here? You see Annex had a school district, and they could not function financially. A few years before I came here in '57, the school district was abolished by the state in 1954.

"At that time the area was divided by Alief, Katy and Houston. In fact, some of the areas had been annexed by Houston. They had to come to Katy because there was a creek there, and there was no bridge over it to pick up the kids and then go back.

"When I came here, we had kids that lived in Annex and Brookshire that played on the football team. Now this was before integration, so we didn't have any black players. All of the black kids were playing at Brookshire. If I am not mistaken, the first black ball player that played for Katy was named Ernie Brown. He eventually went on to become an accountant for Exxon. He was really good young man."

"That's interesting. Coach. I had not yet heard of Ernie

Brown. Thank you for that piece of information. I had uncovered the name of the first black coach who coached at Katy, but I had not heard of the first black player. The coach's name was Clayton Odem. It was a quick reminder to me of how much society had changed. In the entire time that I had been researching *KatyNation*, not once did I think about color. All of the information was so pure and interesting that I had been distracted from the fact that our country had gone through some very challenging times regarding racism.

"The Principal of this school, Mayde Creek, was a black coach over at Memorial Junior High. His name is O. D. Tompkins. He is a fine man. He is almost as good of a man as Roosevelt Alexander."

"Who was Roosevelt Alexander, Coach?"

"Roosevelt Alexander was a gentleman who spent his whole life teaching in the Katy school district. He was the Katy Junior High School Principal when it was over next to the high school. O. D. was a teacher under him.

"Roosevelt lived in Brookshire; he is retired. They named a school after him. The district was late in doing that. They should have done it at lot sooner because he gave his whole life to the Katy School district. He's a fine man."

"Now tell me about coaching back in 1959."

"Back in 1959, there were four coaches. Gordon and I were the high school coaches. I, of course, coached the line. Then, there was Fred Ruland, who was the junior high coach. He is deceased. Then, there was Alfred, also junior high. Only two coaches were what most schools had back then. Back then, we watered the football field. We mowed the field, we marked the field, and we washed the uniforms. On Saturday morning, we used to go into town and buy a bunch of lemons and take the grass stains out of the uniforms."

"That is a great story! I mean. It probably wasn't for

you at that time, but it is a great story to hear about today."
"Yes, we washed uniforms in one area in the gym, and in another section of the gym, we drip-dried the uniforms. It was a very small area at that time."

"I'm sure that it was very humbling back then Coach. As a matter of fact, kids probably take for granted the facilities that they have today. I heard that most schools back then, Coach, didn't have very good lines. If fact, the one thing that Coach Brown said about you was that you were an exceptional line coach."

He smiled, and then pointing at his heart, he said, "Well I coached with this. I want to tell you that when I was in Sam Houston, I worked on construction while I went to school there. Gordon was there a couple years before me. While I was in school, he was playing soldier. I didn't know him until I came to Katy to apply for the job. There was an insurance salesman that was a high school referee. His name was Pete Marueca. One night, Pete kept throwing the flag on my lineman saying, 'Your linemen are jumping.' After the ball game, I went up to him and said, 'My linemen don't jump.' He put his arm around me and said, "Coach I will be over to your place next week, and that will be your week.'"

"Ha, that's funny! So whoever was the home team got the calls?" We had a good laugh.

"My wife went to Stephen F. Austin High School in Houston. She said that Highway 10 ended in Spring Branch and turn into a road. Highway 90 was the main road through Katy at the time. We lost a cheerleader one day. A driver coming in from Houston was blinded by the sunlight and ran through a traffic light, right in front of where that Chevron gas station is today. He ran the light and killed a cheerleader right there. She was on her way to a football game.

"So on Friday evening before the football game, it

was bumper-to-bumper traffic in Katy, mainly because there was only one main road in and out of town. Katy did nothing on Wednesday evening because it was church night. Katy used to be called the City of Churches. You could not schedule anything school wise or otherwise.

"The town was so small that they to used to roll up the sidewalks on Friday nights. As for as football, most the families had a kid that was either in football, the band or cheerleaders. There is an old hardware store where the men used to meet there and talk about football every chance that they got. It was Goyen's Hardware.

"They would meet there, as well, to plan their deer hunting trips. What happened was the fathers would get packed early Friday, go and watch the boys play the ball game, then the kids would ride with the fathers to go deer hunting. Another thing that the school district did then, they had the rodeo and the trail rides. The district felt like it was a great thing for the kids to take a week off from school and go ride the trail rides.

"The school district at the time had seven members. The city of Katy would always reserve a seat on the board for the superintendent of the gas plant that was operating out here at the time. Mr. Taylor had just come home to Katy when the district hired him out of the Coast Guard. He was as tight as three turtles in one shell."

I told Coach Bright that Coach Brown had shared with me a few stories about Mr. Taylor and the tight wallet that he carried for the school district. I also told him that Coach Brown had given me a video of the 1959 state title game itself.

"Well you saw Charlie's touchdown run then. What happened was that Charlie had fumbled the ball, and while picking it back up, the other team's players lost their continuity. Charlie picked that ball up and sprinted like a rabbit in the woods. We had one boy on the team to get a scholarship, Farriel Culpepper.

"His brother John was a preacher. John got killed one Sunday morning while crossing a train track heading to seminary. Now Farriel wasn't the smartest player on the team, but he worked the hardest. I remember that we had hiked the ball all that year on two snap count. Well, we figured that for the playoffs, we would work a couple of plays where we would move on three.

"Well, Farriel kept starting on two and running up the backsides of the center and the guard. Finally, he came back to the huddle where we were and said, 'Coach, I can't think of two things at one time.' So we went back to the two count during the playoffs. Farriel went on to TCU. TCU at the time had a thing for taking country boys and making All-Americans out of them."

"Is Culpepper still here?"

"Yes, I think he is. I think that after he got out of TCU, he went to Duncanville to coach. He was a great fullback for us and a really good kid.

"The summer before 1959, we could not get out coaching with the kids until August 15. Well, in mid-July the backs, and anybody else who wanted, would get out there by themselves and started running the plays. These kids were practicing on their own. It was fun back then. The city was so small that you knew what the parents wanted. We would encourage the kids to get there. The community, being as small as it was, you knew almost everybody there."

Coach then asked me if I knew much about the old high school. I told him that I didn't. He took out a piece of paper and drew a rough floor plan of the school.

"This was the side of the high school. The Principal's office was here. The front door was sort of here. This area here was the high school. This area here was woodshop, In fact, if you look into the movie *Tomboy and Champ*, when the little girl is in the hospital, she was in this room right here, which was an office. This wing here was homemaking; it was about down to here. The rest of the wing was junior high; it was all in the same building.

"Then, you went out this door, and the administration building here was probably four big offices. Then, the gym was over here where we suited out. The cafeteria was here."

"Who was the principal back then, Coach, do you remember?"

"Yes! His name was Jack Rhodes, the one that the stadium was named after. Jack was the first coach here, and he came from Webster. Jack was the Principal, and Taylor was the Superintendent, until Gordon took over.

"Gordon left here and went to Deer Park. Jack was just getting out of college, and Gordon hired Jack to be his line coach there. Then a friend of Gordon's, I want to say Shorty Huges, was coaching at Stephen F. Austin College, and Gordon went there with him as his assistant. Now, I could be wrong on some of these choices, but I think Gordon left the college coaching and went in as Business Manager and Assistant Superintendent of Nacogdoches School District. Then I think that the next place that he went was to Conroe as the Assistant Superintendent; then, he was hired here in Katy as the Superintendent."

"Coach, what was your philosophy back then? You guys had a 10-0 season the year that you went to state."

" Well, we just took it one game at a time. We almost got beat by Waller that year. Waller had this play where they placed ten players on the line, which we were not used to seeing. They were by far our greatest challenge that year."

"Coach let me ask you something, what did you do for players who got hurt back then? Did you have a team doctor?"

"We treated the kids as much as possible. I don't remember when that year, Charlie Peck got his shoulder separated in a game.

"We took him to Doctor Bing the town doctor. Bing took a picture of it and saw how bad it was and said that Charlie was finished for the year. So Charlie's parents came to us and begged us to help. So we took him to the team doctor over at Rice University. What this doctor did was to place a weight in both of Charlie's hands and x-rayed his shoulders to see how far they separated. They said to keep him out of practice for a week and come back and see them. Then the next week, they cleared him to get after it.

"Thad Smith, one of our players wore what they call a octopus knee brace on both knees. He never missed a ball game. It would take him about fifteen minutes to put each one of them on. It had about ten or twelve straps on each one of them. Thad was a tough kid; he played center for us."

"Coach one of the things that I am trying to uncover in the book is what makes Katy football program so much greater than the rest. "

"Well, I'll tell you, even as far back as the 1959 state playoff game, there were people in those stands that had on red and white. Many of these people didn't even have kids and were still at that game. Katy is a special community. I have seen a lot of people move into Katy, but it never changes. Anyway, talking about Katy football stirs me up again."

"I understand, Coach, when I went into Tulley Stadium, I knew in my heart that this was more than just a high school playoff game. I felt that I was seeing a movie in the making. I knew that there had to be something super special to inspire people to create those kinds of numbers to support a local team."

"Let me tell you something about Coach Brown. We developed a game called Tiger Ball. We tried to work the kids out every day to help created a competitive spirit for the kids, things like wrestling for instance. Well, the rule for Tiger Ball was that everyone on the team could catch or throw the football. The only rule was that you could run no more than four to five steps after they caught the pass. Well, Gordon and I would get out there and play with the boys. So, Gordon catches the ball once and drops it. But before he could pick it up, he steps on it. He tore his hamstring so bad that we had to bring a pickup out to load him up to get him home. The next day he had a blue streak all the way down that muscle.

"The whole purpose of the game was to give all the lineman an opportunity to get comfortable with the football. Then we would have wrestling. This was mostly in the off-season. I got to be Head Coach of Katy in 1968 after Coach Brown left. I had one good year and three bad years; then, I got out. The first year we got beat in the bi-district playoffs. The next three years I don't even want to talk about them.

"I asked Taylor for some funds to buy weights so that we could start to developing these kids. You know what he told me? He said that I could buy one set of weights. He was very tight with the money."

"Coach, I have to ask you this, when did you realize that you had a good team back in 1959?"

Coach Bright looked at me and smiled. "About December 24, when we won it all. We had been over to Sugarland a lot. Every time that we would go over for a basketball game, our boys would admire the trophy case that they had. So, we told the boys that every game that you win in the playoffs, we are going to add a foot to your trophy. So, when we had finished and won it all, the boys came in and said, 'Coach, when are we going to order that trophy?'

"So, we went to the tight superintendent, and he said that we could not get it. You can get that gold football from the state, but that is it. So, Gordon and I said that we had to do something; after all we had promised these boys. They did it. We finally came up with the idea of getting that huge picture. There is one at the field house; it's a 4'x8' 'piece of plywood. Hal Carif was a draftsman, and he put in all the kids' names on the picture. So, we got this instead of the large trophy. This turned out even better, because any time a player would come back with his grandkids, he could say, 'There I am, and here's what we did.' So that's what we came up with.

"Here's a quick story that I can share with you about how small the town was. When I first arrived here in Katy, they had the old plug-in telephone system that you see in the old movies, the kind with the one operator at the station board. Well, one night my folks called me from back in East Texas and I was not in. The switchboard operator, I believe her name was Elisabeth Clyant, like every telephone operator, she knew what was going on all over town. Well, she told my folks, if you hang on a moment I believe that I can find him for you. So, it took Elizabeth about three minutes, but she found me over at Coach Brown's home. We were having dinner with them that evening.

"Another thing that I remember was that I never went over to Gordon's house that he was not sitting at a card table, working on some kind of football play. He was a workaholic. It was an old shaky leg card table. He would spend hour after hour at that table.

"There was this kid that was a junior high manager. When we started into the playoffs, I would look up and he would always be there on the bus. Well, just before the state game, I pulled Coach Brown aside and asked him, 'Why did you invite Ray Mangum?' Coach said, 'I didn't invite him, I thought that you did.' Ray was willing to do whatever it took to be a part of this team.

"We had two other managers, Jim and Bill Bone. Jim would have been a great lineman that year, but the year before he was playing softball. He was a catcher; someone was trying to steal home, and they collided at the plate. Well, everything seemed okay. Then, later that year, he started to complain of really bad headaches. It turned out that they had to drill a small hole in his head to release some fluid that was causing pressure on his brain. He had great size and would have been a good player. So, he supported the team as a player in 59.

"One last thing that I want to share with you, Dexter, is this. Most of the times we had kids that didn't have great athletic talent. We found a way to get them involved. What all the kids had, however, was the incredible hearts to play the game of football. That was one of the things that Katy has always been blessed with. Katy has always had kids who have had great hearts. Many times, I often wondered how we were going to get past a team. Those kids never gave up. The Katy Tigers have been doing this for a long time now."

It seemed like every coach that I had spoke of would say the same thing about the Katy football squad. Those two words, great heart, seemed to be another of those common denominators that kept presenting themselves while I researched this book. Though I was becoming aware of this fact, I still needed to locate the source of such a contributing factor, a factor that is embedded into the Katy Tiger football program.

Walking out of Mayde Creek High School that evening, I could not help but think that, in many ways, all of the new schools in Katy ISD were merely extensions of the original Katy High School. Sure, the locations and names were different, but because of the growth of the community, they were forced to evolve. It was easy to surmise that what prevented these other Katy ISD schools from being as successful in football as Katy, was the maturity of the community itself.

The point that Coach Bright help me to understand was what has helped Katy to be so successful was the continual evolution of the community itself. He helped me to better understand that there were countless parts to this machine which represents the Katy Tigers. I was starting to realize that because of Katy's history, change was inevitable.

Stopping for a moment on the campus of Mayde Creek High School before entering my truck and driving off that night, I was greeted by a breeze which reminded me of my stroll around Rhodes Stadium. Even the air was helping to guide me into a direction that would finally take me to my final destination, to the source of KatyNation.

Roosevelt Alexander
(Standing at the Gate)

It seemed as if the name "Roosevelt Alexander" came up every time that I spoke to someone about early Katy. Though this book is about the heritage of the Katy High School football program, I found that another common denominator, which kept reappearing, was the community. Repeatedly, I am reminded of what this community has done to help resurrect an ailing football program. It became very obvious through Katy's history that the community and administration had found ways to resuscitate the football program when it was needed.

When you see the thousands of people who fill the stands today, you have to ask yourself a number of questions. First, how did this all happen? Secondly, can a community's energy redirect the course and the outcome of a football game? Any sportscaster today will tell you that momentum can change the completion of any sporting contest. The big question, however, is "How does it work." Where does it come from? Can it be bought over the counter, and how much does it cost?

While thinking about the community's involvement in the success of Katy's football program, I wondered about the importance of the seeds planted by the KISD administration in the early years. Could it be that the countless unknown faces of men and women of Katy's past might be partially responsible for some of the success of a football program that is second-to-none?

Coach Gordon Brown was the first to echo the name

Roosevelt Alexander in my ears. He said, "You can't write about the Katy community without including Roosevelt Alexander." When I first heard him say that, it honestly never occurred to me that he was talking to me about a black man. The more I heard the name, the more I wondered about this person's contribution to the Katy community. Over and over, his name rang in my ears. I could see that these once-very-important members of the Katy community had a reason for sharing the name Roosevelt Alexander. I owed it to them to turn my research in that direction.

One of the things that I have always said about sports in America is that it has a remarkable ability to cross racial lines and create serious change. Throughout the history of any city or town, this fact has repeated itself over and over again, giving communities all across this nation an opportunity to change philosophies, ideals, and old concepts about race and humanity. There is no doubt that America's cities and towns have made great strides in this area. In my heart, I feel that there is no greater ally in this cause than high school athletics.

Roosevelt Alexander, like many other people of color, found a way to become a part of this special community of Katy, Texas. He arrived here in a time when school sports had not yet been given the authority to help abolish racism.
Fortunately, it was not difficult to located Roosevelt. I found him still living in the Katy community that he helped to build. The 411 operator gave me the listing, and there I was again, standing at the door of time, seconds away from crossing over into that special dimension of Katy's heritage which keeps reminding me how blessed that I am to have the opportunity to write this book.

The phone rang six times. Expecting to get an answering service, I was surprised when a soft voice picked up the phone. "Yes ma'am, my name is Dexter Clay. I am not sure if I have the right Alexander. I am looking for the Roosevelt Alexander who worked for the Katy school district."

"Well, I think that you have the right Alexander."
"I'm writing a book of the history of Katy High School football, and your husband's name keeps appearing."

" Well, he never coached at Katy, but he is as big of a part of this community as anyone that you will find."

"Your name, please?"

"Oh, I'm Gracie."

"It is a pleasure to meet you, Gracie." After I gave her a little more information about *KatyNation*, she told me the best time to reach her husband. I left my number, thanked her for her time, and asked her to please have her husband call me.

It was about an hour and a half later when the phone rang. Ha! "Mr. Alexander, thank you for returning my call."
I learned in that phone call that he was born in East Oakwood in Leon County. In 1950, he graduated from St Paul-Shiloh High School. He set off for college at the then-all-black college, Prairie View A&M. In 1954 after the Korean War, he found himself in the Army as part of a regiment responsible for maintaining communication for the 5th Airborne Division. Afterwards, he returned to Prairie View to complete his Masters degree. He applied for teaching jobs at Lagrange, Lubbock, Katy and Midland School Districts.

When Roosevelt Alexander arrived in Katy back in 1958, he carried his seeds of wisdom to a then-segregated community. At the time, black students were bused to Brookshire, so that is where Mr. Alexander started his career. Though he would eventually spread his wisdom throughout the Katy community, at the time, he was reminded of the evolution of our nation. Roosevelt's career started at an all-black school located on Danover Road in Brookshire.

In that day, one teacher taught first and second grade; another taught third and fourth grade, another taught fifth and sixth grade, and the principal taught seventh and eighth grade. All of these students were located in one building. Roosevelt started out with fifth and sixth grade and coached both the boys' and the girls' basketball and track teams.

I was still a little unclear just why the principle figures in the Katy football past insisted that I interview Mr. Alexander. The answer came in my first telephone conversation with him. He said, "I remember following the Katy Tigers in their 1959 march towards the State Championship game. I did not actually see the Tigers in the regular season play. I remember walking up to the gate to buy a ticket, and I was kindly told that I could_buy a ticket but I could not enter through that particular gate. I was told that there was a special section of stands that were available to sit in for blacks only. I looked at the person at the gate, and I was angry, but I said, 'No thank you. I don't live my life that way,' and turned and walked off."

Then Mr. Alexander said something that made me understand why he was so highly endorsed to be a part of this book. "Today I am responsible for all the monies gathered at the gates of KISD football programs. Each Friday and Saturday night, I am reminded of the evidence of change that has developed in our community." I knew then what the others were trying to share with me. This man obviously has the character of what it takes to be a part of the Katy community. I needed not to ask any more questions about what Roosevelt Alexander's role was in this book.

It was a late afternoon Saturday, when my opportunity came around to meet with Mr. Alexander. The Tigers happened to be playing that evening against the new kids on the block, the Morton Ranch Mavericks. I arrived at Jack Rhodes stadium about 5:30 p.m. The place felt like a hive with a number of worker bees preparing for the queen to arrive. Schools buses were pulling up and dropping off band members. Parents were getting their assignments for the evening. Security people were preparing themselves for the evening crowds. Coaches and trainers from both teams were "dressing" their side of the field preparing for battle. There was no question that something very special was about to take place here.

I walked around and up the ramp to the field house. I ran into Bubba Fife, one of Katy's Assistant Athletic Directors. "Oh, hi, Bubba, it's good to see you."

"Hey, Dexter. It's good to see you."

"Thank you," I said. "I'm interviewing Roosevelt Alexander this evening."

"Oh, Mr. A. He's in his office. Go on in."

"All right, I will see you later on." "So they call him Mr. A around here," I thought to myself. There was even more activity going on inside the field house. Referees were preparing to meet before the night's game. Volunteers and other supporters of the event were getting ready. In the center of all the excitement, I found Mr. A. Seeing him for the first time reminded me of my grandfather. I was only six when I first met him, and then he passed away two days later. I still remember that look of elegance and distinction that my grandpa had. It seemed to embrace Mr. A's being as well. It is a look the confidence from someone who knows that he has lived life and conquered all of its challenges.

I worked my way in the Mr. A's office, weaving through those standing around getting him to "sign off" release forms for this and that.

"Mr. Alexander," extending my hand, "I'm Dexter Clay, author of *KatyNation*."

"Oh Dexter, hello, I'm glad that you could make it." I could see that he had just finished a late lunch. How he managed to eat with all the activity all around him was interesting to see. I knew that this interview was not going to be the quiet one I had had with most of my other subjects. That was okay. What make this process so exciting is not knowing what is about to happen. Just adapting and enjoying the ride is the key to researching for a book. I was simply happy to be there.

Reaching into my satchel, pulling out my recorder, I noticed that I was beginning to wear off some of the paint on the "Play" button. Once again, I set it on the deck and smiled because I knew that I was taking that trip back into time again. This time this trip was from a black perspective.
I realized that Mr. A had the Michigan football game playing. This explained why the TV's monitor mesmerized a couple of guys. I didn't mind, so I began my questioning, after turning the volume of the set down just a little.

"Mr. A," I asked, "I would like to get started from your beginning in Katy."

"Well, like I said, I arrived in Katy in 1958. I lived in Brookshire. Katy was segregated at the time. I taught at Kilpatrick Elementary School, which is still there. Kilpatrick went from grades one through eight. I was at Kilpatrick from 1958 to 1970. In 1970, that's when they fully integrated.

"There were three families with a total of five students that integrated Katy High School in 1964 after the Supreme Court's ruling came down. They refused to have their kids be bused to Cy-Fair High School, which was further away when Katy was so close. What happened was that Katy didn't have a black high school at the time, and Brookshire didn't have a white high school. So the white kids from Brookshire were bused to Katy High, and Katy's black kids were bused to Brookshire.

"In 1970, all districts were forced by the government to comply with the 1964 ruling."

"Mr. A, was there a lot of negative energy here in the community." I looked closely into his eyes for his response.

"Yes, there was some," he said, almost not wanting to show that he was disappointed by Katy's past. "But let me say this, as bad as it was in most places, it was very minor here in Katy. It was not nearly as bad as it was in, say, some of the other larger cities like Chicago or Boston. I can honestly say that Katy has such a quality community that they made the adjustments. A few minor things but really nothing to be alarmed about."

"Mr. A, how did you handle all this?"

"I think that one of the things about a Christian community is that you don't carry the heart and mentality of the rest of the world. [During] any adversities that I experienced at that time in my life, I said to myself that it would not pay me to come away from life's challenges with a negative outlook. You cannot accomplish your goals of what you want to do in life if you go around with a huge chip on your shoulders. I just refused to do that. Now don't get me wrong, I stood up for what I thought was right.

"Like I told you that game where I was told that I could not go into the same gate...."

"You don't remember what game that was do you? Did you know that there was going to be a confrontation?"

"Yes I did, but I had to try. It was a part of the mentality of the time period. Our business manager Mr. Fussell warned me. He had given me tickets for the game but explained to me that I would not be allowed to go into the same gate as the whites. I was also told that there was a certain section that I had to sit in as well. He said, 'I just want to warn you, Roosevelt.' He was a good man, and he was trying to warn me about what I might encounter. He is still alive today; he's in his nineties."

Immediately, my mind raced back to the Fussell funeral that I had gone to earlier in my research for the book. I watched as my memory recalled the little old man filled with grief being helped out of the back of the funeral home during the wake.

"What a small world this is I thought to myself. No matter where we are from or how different we think that we are. Life will find a way to show us that we are of the same family, whether we like it or not."

"Mr. Fussell and I served on the credit union board together just a few years back. He was the one that organized the credit union, as a matter of fact. The credit union that we have in Katy…well, we have seven branches from all over. One in Fort Bend, one in Sugar Land, one in Brenham and College Station. We have seven of them. Well, Fussell was the organizer, starting out with twelve people…started out with $65.00, now we are over three hundred million."

"I'm sure that those were difficult times back then. I'm sure that you had friends that took a different approach than the one that you took. How did you maintain your focus?"

"Again, I simply tried to focus on what I had control over. One of the things that my mother used to say was, 'Treat everybody the way that you would like to be treated, Roosevelt.' She said that all the time while I was growing up. She said you have to learn to accept people for who they are. It was more or less my spiritual foundation that helped me to live that reasoning and not just talk about it.

"You know this used to be called the City of Churches?

I believe that this helped to create a special foundation for this community. After we integrated in the 1970s, I still had challenges. My biggest challenge was winning the parents over. There were some who felt that I was not qualified to teach their kids. So showing them that I was qualified was constantly with me in those early '70s."

"Was there a key to that? How did you change their minds?"

"They key was proving to them that I was qualified by teaching the kids. The kids were my biggest supporters because they were learning. The fact that the kids were learning began to help silence those who opposed me. The kids became the end results, and that is what ultimately changed the minds of my opposition. I had to work twice as hard because of that, but that ultimately helped me become a better teacher.

"The Principal at that time was Garland McMeans. Garland was very supportive to me in those days. October 25, 1998, they had the dedication of a new elementary school, Roosevelt Alexander. It was at that time that I truly felt thankful for my road taken in Katy, a road that presented me with a lot of people who supported me along the way. This is a good community to live in.

"The most important thing that you have to learn is life is about timing as well. We had a superintendent here that, as long as he was here, I was not going anywhere. I had to deal with that and not allow that to change my attitude about the community that I was learning to love. Then that situation changed, and the new superintendent helped to pave the way for me to accelerate my career. That was where patience on my part had to come in to play."

"Who was that superintendent that help open the door for you Mr. A?"

"Oh, his name was Gordon Brown."

"You mean Coach Brown?" I said. "I didn't realize that he was also the Superintendent of Katy as well." Then I smiled. It all made sense why I was there in Mr. A's office. Coach Brown was trying to tell me that there was something that would have been missing if I had missed out on this interview.

"Gordon was the one that won the state championship in 1959." I smiled because Mr. A did not realize that Coach Brown had told me about him, and that, in a roundabout way, Coach was still looking after him.

"Mr. A, how about the 80s, how were they for you?"

"Well, like I said, my career accelerated. My biggest supporters were always my parents. But in the 80s, a lot of the kids that I once taught started to come back to express the fact that I had been instrumental in their lives as a teacher. I became Principal of the junior high in 1981, up until I retired in 1993."

"So, indirectly, you were responsible for the football players in Katy, even before they got to the high school?"

"Yes, I never looked at it that way before. But I guess that you are right. At one time Katy Junior High was responsible for all of the athletes that went to Katy High, but then West Memorial started to feed into Katy High School as well."

"Mr. A, what do you think was the most memorable moment in your career?" Sitting back in his chair, I could see him going back into his past to bring to the surface the response to my question.

"Most of my real rewards have come from the kids that I taught. The times that they would come back and express their gratitude for my involvement in their lives. As a teacher, it truly doesn't get any better than that. For instance, I have a letter and tape from a young lady that I taught math in Junior

High. Her name was Marcy McConnell. She's in Fort Bend now. She teaches science over at the junior high school. She sent a letter over to the credit union because she didn't know how to reach me.

"She said, 'I don't know if you remember me, but I was just awarded Secondary Teacher of the Year. I just wanted you to know that it was because of you that I became a teacher.' The next year she had an opportunity to speak to all the teachers and administrators in her district, and she expressed the fact that I was instrumental to her success. Well, I had friends call me up and tell me that I been mentioned. They all said, 'I wish that you could have been there.' They said that Marcy McConnell spoke highly of me.

"To me when a ex-student says that you made a difference in his life, that is the most rewarding thing that can happen to you. To see those wonderful little kids come back as adults and acknowledge you for your efforts is a wonderful thing to experience. Coaches touch a lot of kids' lives, as well. What they offer kids in their lives is priceless.

"I had another young man that wrote a letter to the school board to have Cinco Ranch named in my honor. I have a lot of good memories here. Katy has been really good for me."

"When did this position that you have today present itself?"

"Well, let's see, it was back in the '70s; a man by the name of Jack Rhodes who was the athletic director, and he used to be the coach of Katy High School.... Anyway he came to me and another young man by the name of Mike Griffin and asked us if we would work the gates for Katy High School until he could find someone. We hesitated about it. We were only getting three dollars a night. Well, at three dollars, we knew that he was not going to find anybody.

Anyway, we both decided that we would both work the gates.

"Mike worked until he became Assistant Principal of Katy High School. Then he quit, and I continued on. When they built this stadium was in 1981. I remember because my daughter graduated from the stadium." "How many children do you have?"

"I have three daughters: Griselda, Cassandra, and my oldest Deshauda. Griselda was the homecoming queen. So, when this stadium opened up out here, they asked me if I would continue to do this."

As I completed my interview with Mr. A, I could hear the National Anthem being played by the Katy High School band. I was glad that I had made this stop into Katy's past. I had just spent some time with a real piece of history. I thanked Mr. A, for his time, and we found ourselves alone in his office, which was surprising, because through the entire interview, people who knew him would pop in and say, "Hello!" Now that the game was about to start, everyone seemed to disappear outside.

The two of us found ourselves standing there, looking through the large glass picture window, which overlooks the north end of Rhodes Stadium. I smiled to myself thinking that his office was actually the best place to view the game in the house. Life does have a funny way of bringing things to life. Here was a man who, during a certain time period in society, could not even get into the gate of a Katy game. Now, that same man found himself responsible for all those same monies in a different time period.

A man who was once told that he had to sit in a special section of the stadium was now given the opportunity to view each game from the best seat in the house. The two of us stood at the window, not saying a word as the Katy Tigers kicked the ball high into the air. In that moment, I knew that we were not alone because somewhere in the sands of time, this moment had been written long before we got there. In further research on Mr. A, I came across some letters that had been written by ex-students of his. I thought I would share a few with you. I realize that there is possibility that some teachers might find themselves questioning whether or not they are fully appreciated for all the countless hours of dedication devoted to better educate the world's children. These letters that I uncovered are my way of saying to you that your work never goes unnoticed.

"Mr. Alexander, Hi! I thought you might be interested to know what one of your former students thinks of you. Thank you for touching his life so profoundly Hope to see you soon.

Judy Coen"

Dr. Don Stacy
P.O. Box 159
Katy, TX 77492-0159

Dear Dr. Stacy,
I am truly excited to learn that K.I.S.D. has decided to build a fourth high school. This undoubtedly reflects the growth of the greater Katy area and the emphasis placed on a quality education. The new high school should be named after someone who exemplifies the pursuit for a quality education, and I wholeheartedly believe that Roosevelt Alexander is worthy of the honor.
Mr. Alexander served diligently as a teacher, assistant principal, and principal for over thirty years. During this time, he dedicated his life to the education of students.

155

Mr. Alexander had the unique ability to relate to students of all different backgrounds and influence them in a positive manner. He won numerous awards and honors during his teaching and administration career and the admiration of the students and teachers alike.

On a personal note, I would like to add that Mr. Alexander made a difference in my life. He provided strong leadership while I was a student at Katy Jr. High and was a great role model. He always greeted me with a smile and a handshake, and he constantly challenged me to reach my potential. He also cared about his students after they moved on, as he came to my graduation party last spring. I can honestly say that Mr. Alexander's influence as an educator is the main reason that I am an honors student at the University of Texas.

To conclude, I believe that Roosevelt Alexander's excellence as an educator in K.I.S.D. more than qualifies him to have a high school named in his honor. He represents all that a quality high school should represent, the pursuit of an excellent quality of education for students. Sincerely,

Jason Coen
KHS Class of '96

Here is another example of respect for Mr. Alexander:

Mr. Roosevelt Alexander
Katy Junior High
6501 Highway Blvd.
Katy, Texas 77450

Dear Mr. Alexander:

156

Sharon and I want to thank you and your staff for the many positive things that have happened to our son Mark during his career at Katy Junior High. You have truly made junior high an enjoyable experience for him. In fact, he doesn't want to leave Katy Junior high. I think that is a real tribute to your staff and the positive climate they have established for your students.
Thanks, again, we truly appreciate the job you have done.

Sincerely,

James Tays
Principal
West Memorial Junior High School

...and another example:

Mr. Alexander
     Thanks for all the wonderful memories I have had at KJH. If there was one word I could say that describes how I feel about you, it is respect. I have so much respect for you and the way you handle the students you come in contact with on a daily basis. I can speak for my entire family to say - Our best wishes to you - We want to keep in touch- God bless you.

  Your friend forever,
Lynn Yates

…and a final example:

Zion Hill Baptist Church
P.O. Box 4488
Brookshire, Texas 77423

October 14, 1998

Mr. Roosevelt Alexander
Zion Hill Baptist Church
P.O. Box 1488
Brookshire, Texas 77423

Dear Mr. Alexander:

The Zion Hill Memorial Scholarship Committee would like to express their sincere gratitude to you for making the scholarship fund a success. We are thankful to you for keeping account of the funds generated by this committee.

Thank you for the dedication that you have shown the boys and girl of the Brookshire and Katy communities. Your service will be engraved in all of our lives. We are particularly pleased that Katy I.S.D. has named a school in your honor. You are truly worthy of this honor.

Again, we thank you for your unselfish service to the member of Zion Hill and the community.

Yours in Christ,

Hearlean Hart, Chairperson
Scholarship Fund

I realized as I closed the folder, which held over forty letters, that I had been circling around the KatyNation community. This man was one of the many fine individuals that the Katy community had managed to attract. I recognized that these were elements that opposing fans of Katy Tiger football never had a chance to see as they walked away from another unfavorable scoreboard, shaking their heads and wondering how Katy manages to beat them again. They never imagined that Katy's success started way before the two teams took the football field.

Mr. A's voice is just one of many who have helped to nurture a community of champions. Katy's football success goes far beyond the Friday night lights. Seemingly countless invisible characters have helped to prepare this community for the success that many of us see today. Like the Native Americans who once crossed these plains, the presence of those characters still echo in the ears of opponents. One thing is for sure, you cannot argue with the fact that something mighty powerful is happening in this community, and it simply didn't happen overnight.

Looking In the Eyes of a Tiger

Coach Mike Johnston

It was the day before the 2006 spring Red and White Game of the Katy Tigers. I happened to be in Katy that evening and thought that I would drop over to Rhodes Stadium after hearing that the Tigers were having dress rehearsal for the game the following day. I got there at the close of the practice session, only to see the coaches walking off the field.

What I saw next was something that to this day has raised the hair on the back of my neck. There, at the north end of the field under the goal post, was the entire Tiger team. There were no coaches or teachers or parents. The young boys were sharing their internal concerns about the team. It was one of the most organized and sincere discussions that I had ever heard from a group of any kind. Just when I thought this was one of the greatest events that I had ever seen, one on the young men stood and closed the team discussion with a prayer.

By this time, I had a lump in my throat. I saw a group of young men, without any adult supervision, showcasing the kind of leadership that, quite frankly, I can never recall seeing before. This was more evidence of the Katy community implanting the spirit of champions in its youth. I saw true leadership that afternoon. I saw an example from which our senators and congressmen in Washington could learn. Young men were discussing issues which concerned them without screaming and pointing fingers of who was right and who was wrong. As they finished and jogged off the field, I felt the presence of young warriors going into battle as they passed by me.

I stood there looking at the now-empty field, still in a state of disbelief. I had just seen for myself the spirit of Katy's heritage in the eyes of the young Tigers, and I felt extremely humbled. I turned around to look back towards the field house and saw Coach Joseph standing with another man. Walking towards them, I recognized that he was standing with none other than Mr. Legend himself, Coach Mike Johnston.

I reached out my hand to Coach Joseph. "Hi, Coach, it's good to see you." I then turned to Coach Johnston as Coach Joseph introduced him to me. "Wow," I said, "I'm standing between two legends."

Coach Johnston smiled and said, "Well, like Bum Phillips used to say, 'All good legends are usually dead ones.'" We all laughed. Then Coach Joseph told Coach Johnston that I was the person who was writing the book about the history of Katy football. It was there that I gave my little presentation speech to Coach Johnston. One of the other coaches stepped outside to get Gary's attention, leaving me alone with Coach Johnston.

Coach Johnston's presence told me that he was still very much a part of the community energy that fueled Katy's football program. "Coach, I would love to get your thoughts about this program that you have worked so hard to help build."

"Well, I'm going to be a little busy for the week, but after that, you call me, and I will put aside some time to tell you what I can."

That was my first meeting with Coach Mike Johnston. Leaving the stadium that evening, I felt blessed once again. Every person whom I met regarding this program had been very positive.

Throughout the depths of this community is a spirit of righteousness that those who were here before have conveyed to their descendants. I was not writing about the success of a high school football team here. I had stumbled across something far greater than a weekend movie. Unfolding before my eyes was something that the whole world needed to know about, something that could change the ideals of a nation in a positive way.

KatyNation was starting to portray more than just the success of a football program from Katy's heritage. This book was starting to unearth the diagram that helped to make a community stand out from the rest.

It was about ten days later when I touched base with Coach Johnston. We agreed to meet at the field house over at Katy High School around noon that Thursday. I didn't know it at the time, but in the next five hours, I would look in to the heart of a Tiger and be changed forever.

Coach Johnston and I somehow managed to arrive in the parking lot at the same time. As he got out of his car, he looked back to see me walking up. "Hey," he said. "It's good to see you."

"It's good to see you, Coach." As we walked toward the building, a feeling of comfort settled in my bones. In each interview that I conducted, I never felt like a stranger. Each person seemed to prepare a friendship for me so that our meetings were never awkward. With each step that we took towards the door, I felt that I was about to have a conversation with an old friend.

Coach Johnston still carries the seal of approval around Katy. We walked in past everyone, and people acknowledged him as if he were a celebrity. He took me back into the coaches' office where I was in total awe! Even though Coach

Joseph had a separate office, there was another large room, and this room looked like serious work was being done there.

The room was filled with about fifteen to twenty separate stations. Each workstation contained state-of-the-art computers and monitors as if a military task force were researching and preparing for a powerful air or ground strike on the enemy. On a few on the monitors, I could that defenses were being dissected and offenses perfected. Even though the room was empty, there was no doubt that these were the stations where generals were preparing for battle.

Coach Johnston pulled up a chair for me. The monitor at that station had a Katy Tiger player breaking through an opposing offense to make a sack on the running back. "The coaches are in a meeting, so we can talk here until they come in."

One experience that made this place so impressive was a visit I made to my old high school a few days prior to this interview. There, gathered around one old television set, were ten coaches trying to view the highlights of a game film. If I wasn't mistaken, it was the same old television set that I used to watch thirty years before. The difference between the two offices was as plain as day and night. The byproduct of winning truly created different surroundings, and here was the perfect example.

Granted, I knew in my heart that there were a lot of elements to winning that I was viewing as well. One that helped Katy stand out in the crowd was its community support. You cannot deny that the contributions from Katy's community and boosters have a dramatic effect on the success of its program. It was extremely evident in the difference between the two high school offices.

Unfortunately, many school districts and their booster club patrons cannot afford the luxuries enjoyed in Katy.

However, I do know that even one winning season can open some otherwise closed pocketbooks.

I wasn't really sure just where to start the interview with Coach Johnston. I had learned along the way to allow each interview to unfold because it seems to create a more natural flow. Coach Johnston asked me if I would like any coffee. I declined, and he began to open the windows of time.

"My coaches would always tease me and ask me how I could drink coffee when it was ninety-eight degrees outside. I have been drinking this stuff since I was twelve years old."

"So, you're not into that designer coffee like Starbucks."

"No, my wife Donna is. I am a regular, leaded coffee drinker. She and her friends hang up there at Starbucks after they go to the gym. They do their knitting there and drink those designer coffees, like you called them.

"Donna is retired. She retired from Katy ISD at the same time that I did. She is the perfect coach's wife. We met back at SFA, and we have been together ever since. Her patience and dedication to my career and me has been second to none. She was good. She was used to moving, having been a preacher's kid. When I say that I have been blessed, I mean it. I see it through her love for me and our family."

"Coach, when did you arrive here at Katy High School?"

"I came to Katy from Abilene High School back in 1980 as the Offensive Coordinator. Bill Branum was the Head Coach of Katy at the time. Two years later, Bill went into the administration, and I became the Head Coach. To be honest with you, I think I got the job by default. I really don't think that the list of applicants was very long. Bill had been the Head Coach since Gordon left."

"When did you first meet Coach Brown?" I asked.

"I came in contact with Gordon back when I played football at Stephen F. Austin. Gordon was the Offensive

Coordinator at the time. Gordon took the head coaching job over at Nacogdoches. I worked underneath Gordon for four years, and then went to Beaumont, and then to Abilene.

"I was at Katy two years before I got the head coaching job. I think that I was on a very short list. Not a whole lot of coaches cared to move out to Katy back then. I hired Gary Joseph in the summer of 1982 as the Secondary Coach. I have to be honest with you. Gary was the best coach that I had ever been around. Also, I had Ray Biles with me back then. We had some very tough years. I didn't have a lot of allies on my side in those early years. But I will tell you that the ones that I did have, like Bill Haskett, were sent from up above. Bill truly had my back in those lean years.

"You see, today, most people think that a successful program happens overnight. The fact is that true success, the kind of success that Katy is having today, came from people who believed in what we were doing, even when the scoreboard was not to our favor. Most people today don't realize that Bill Haskett is as much a part of Katy's football success as any coach out there on the field. He simply believed in us and what we were doing in a time when others didn't. If he had given up on us, like most had back then, there would have been another chapter to the Katy Tiger story.

"Success in a high school program starts with the head. And I don't mean the coaches. There are a lot of little things that people never see that help to add to the success of a program. Back after 1997, I spoke with Robert Blankenship, one of the administrative assistants. Well, long story short, Robert was the one that allowed me to hire Connie, Gary's secretary. It might not seem to have been a big thing to most people, but Connie was a lifesaver. She helped to free me up from so much of the paperwork that was required of the athletic coordinator. I could actually start to spend more time with my family again. But before Connie came along, I was so bogged down in paperwork, I had limited time to spend on anything, and that included coaching. Sometimes winning is making little adjustment along the way.

"Going back to some of the early coaches when I was at Katy, I was blessed to be around some pretty good men. All of them who I knew would someday be coaching at 5A programs. Like Gary, he interviewed for a lot of coaching jobs back then. I used to tell Gary that I always believed that there was a reason that he was not being hired. It was because he was supposed to be here in this job, Gary's response was, 'I don't want your job, Mike.'

"'I know that you don't want it. You have been here for a long time; these people and this community know you. They understand and know how much you care for these kids.' What a great coach!

"'You can be yourself here; you can be Gary Joseph.' Everything truly worked out well. I was so pleased and thrilled that things turned out the way they did.

"I knew Gary. You don't work with someone for over twenty years without understanding what makes him happy. Gary was used to the big games.

"You see Gary performs at his best in big-game situations."

At that time, I mentioned that Coach Joseph has a very unique demeanor: quiet, but very powerful, as if he were playing chess or something.

"Let me tell you something about Gary. Gary is always a play or two ahead of you, mentally. Monday and Tuesday, he would have his head buried in that computer," he said, pointing at the area where Coach Joseph used to sit.

"You could not even talk to him Monday or Tuesday of

every week. Gary is the kind of coach that can get in your head. He knows what you are going to call before even you know what play that you are going to call. He is as strong a student of the game as I have ever seen. I tell you, I mean it; he is as good as I have ever seen. In fact, I recommended Gary to a number of college teams. I would have hated to lose him, but I knew that he was that good.

"Fortunately for me, colleges were more into appearances than taking on a great coach that was coaching high school football. I have always felt blessed to have had Gary a part of my coaching staff over the years."

I recognized genuine sincerity in Coach Johnston's words as he spoke of Coach Joseph. One point that I had uncovered about the three principle coaching figures in Katy's football history was that all three seem to be incredibly humble men, men who were not afraid to acknowledge the presence of God. They all seemed to show God's presence through examples rather than by shouting from the coaching pulpit.

They appeared to credit those around them more than themselves. It was a unique characteristic that I found to be refreshing in today's world. It was obvious that the energy from these men had manifested itself throughout the history of the Tigers' program, as if these coaches had worked to be conduits between the Heavenly Father and the Tigers of *KatyNation*. This was becoming increasingly clear to me.

During my research, I stumbled across a story that I could not wait to discuss with Coach Johnston. It was a story that I'm sure that many who have followed the Katy Tigers the last few years knew well. I was simply trying to find the right time to ask Coach about it. Fortunately for me, Coach Johnston mentioned something that opened the door to the Tigers of 1998.

This was the year that the Tigers were told that they had to get off the bus that was headed to the 1998 5A Championship game. I had just asked Coach the question about what makes the community of Katy so special. When I did, the volume of my interview was turned up five decibels.

"I think that this community loves it when they see kids go out and play 'inspired.' They seem to feed off of the fact that these kids are playing hard football. But the one thing that really brought this community together was the time that I had to take their kids off of the buses. In 1998, we got disqualified. It was at that time in my career that I saw this community evolve into a community of champions.

"It was a tough holiday for us. You and I have talked about the spiritual aspect of things, but this was the ultimate test of the will of a community...the things that you didn't read in the newspapers...things like what came out of all this situation.

"I had known on that Thursday before that weekend's scheduled game about the possibility that we couldn't play. It was before that Thursday's practice at Rhodes stadium that I found out. I was told that we might have a problem with the forgery of a player's grade. Well, I just knew that this could not be true. I had all the kids' grades in my desk.

"I only shared the news with one other coach. Ironic enough, the whole situation was brought to our attention by a teacher who had seen a kid on the field a couple of weeks before. I had all transcripts at my disposal, and I was under the impression that everything was in order. So what was difficult for me personally was the fact that I had been carrying this knowledge inside of me for several hours now.

"When I got back from practice, I found that the principal was sitting in my office; this is when I was informed that we indeed had a forgery.

"The next morning, we tried to get a hold of the Katy Athletic Department, but most everyone was out for the holiday season. The secretary told me that she would get the message out, and she would get right back to me as soon as she could. Once they got back with me, they told me that they were checking into the matter, and that for right now, we should continue forward and be prepared to play.

"The next morning before we were about to leave to go to the state championship game, I was called over to the Administration Building. I had to walk to get over there because the school parking lot was filled with buses and cars and families prepared to take off for the game. Stepping into the administration office, I felt that there something was very wrong. The energy in the whole room was so thick you could have cut it with a knife. It was there that I was told by our principal that we had definitely been disqualified. I remembered my heart dropping to the floor when I heard the news. I, of all people, knew just how hard those kids had worked to have the opportunity to be on those buses.

"I then called back over and told Gary to get the kids off the bus and take them to the team room. I told big Chad not to let any parents in and that I would be over in a few minutes. Each step that I took towards the team room made my heart beat faster. Opening the door to the team room was one of the toughest things that I have ever had to do in all my years as a football coach.

"There was only one thing that I could do, that was to be direct and straightforward with those kids. I told them that Katy High School had been disqualified from the State Championship game. That we had broken a state law, 'No pass, No play'! I really felt bad for the kids.

"As I looked into the eyes of the young Tigers, the reality of what I was saying started to grow. I think that I felt the worst for our seniors. We had fifty two seniors in the group that year."

I watched as Coach Johnston's energy level dropped. By telling me the story, he stumbled across that time in his life, only to become disappointed by the situation again. Coach Johnston continued to recall the unpleasant account of how a young player had forged a grade, which resulted in the team being disqualified from competition.

"To this day, I always felt that they should have at least let us play the game, and if they felt that we should be disqualified later, then take it away from us. The worst thing that you can do to a competitor is not to give him the chance to compete

"Instead, MacArthur High School was called in under very short notice. They had not been mentally ready to be in the championship game, so they got themselves blown out of the game. I don't believe that it was fair to MacArthur or Midland Lee. I had heard that Midland Lee was also upset about it. Midland was prepared to play us, not MacArthur. Again, if they felt that we broke the UIL rule, 'No Pass No Play,' then fine, disqualify us after the ball game was over. Our kids worked hard to get there.

"Anyway that weekend, it was pretty bad after having the meeting with the kids. Sunday morning, I'm walking to Sunday school before church, and people are walking up to me saying, 'Bronston Carroll spoke at church, and he was great.' Bronston was a running back and one of our team captains. He spoke to the congregation earlier. I asked what Bronston had done. Apparently, unknown to me after all the coaches had gone, Bronston called a meeting with all the players and told them that they all had to be careful how they react to [the player who forged the grade]. How we reacted, he said, would send a message both to the students and to the community.

"This was the quality of leadership that can be found in the kids of the Katy community. Last I heard, he was just finished playing at the Naval Academy and now he was out on a submarine somewhere in the Atlantic.

"Bronston was a tough kid, too. He broke his ankle in the second round of the playoffs. He plays on that ankle the rest of the year. He also breaks and dislocates three of his middle toes on his left foot in our semifinal game. He was going to play in the state game with a steel metal plate in his left foot and a broken ankle on his right foot. The unusual thing is that the kid never took anything for the pain. Talk about being tough. That kid was extraordinary example of being tough. Great kid, one of the best leaders that I have ever been around.

"You know, I believe, as Christians, when you are at the very lowest, at the very bottom of the pit of defeat, I believe that an experience like what this community went through...somehow, God intends for great things to come out of that. This community was tested and answered the call that year. When people speak of a community coming together in a time of despair...it was this episode that made me understand that I had become a part of something greater than just a football program.

"Later on in the new year that January, the recruiting for the new coaches was taking place. Well, a few of the coaches came up to me and said, 'Whatever happened to that kid? Whatever happened to that kid?' I would tell them, 'Oh, he is up in that building over there.' 'You've got to be kidding?' they would respond. 'You mean that the kid is still going to school here?' None of the young coaches ever caught on. I had one of the older coaches tell me. He says, 'You know what, Coach? It really says a lot about the spirit of the community in Katy.' I said, 'Yeah, it really does! The kid messed up, and the community had a forgiving spirit.' The kid went on and graduated from here. To my knowledge, I don't recall that he ever had any problems. It was just like the kid's father told him, 'If you had been in any other community, it could have been a lot worse.'

"It was this situation that made me realize how attached this community was to the program. It was very difficult around here in the winter of 1998. For a while there, you could feel people walking on eggshells. For some reason, it was a few weeks where it was literally cloudy outside, gray and cold."

"Coach, that truly is a remarkable story."

"Yes this is a special community. There was a young lady who played in the band who wrote a wonderful article that year. I still have the article. The message of the article was that you can not defeat the spirit of the Katy Tigers.

"So in 1999, our kids came back with a sense of motivation, not negative but positive. They wanted to come back and recapture the integrity and pride. To me that was one of the neat things. There was not a lot of finger pointing and placing-the-blame. It made me proud to be their coach.

"Our 1999 team did not have the talent as the 1997 team had, but they really wanted to prove that they could be just as good as the '97 team."

"Coach," I asked, "do you think that motivation is a key factor in the consistency of the Katy Tigers program?"

"I think that it is an underlying factor. Yes, these kids want to live up to the winning tradition that was planted back with Coach Gordon Brown. In 1999, we went back again and got beat by Garland in the championship game. In 2000, we went and beat John Tyler for it. In 2001, we had some internal problems. Pride got a hold of us a little bit; we got a little arrogant. But I must say that we got taken out by a pretty good group, too. Old Madison and Vincent Young took us out in the second round. In 2002, we lost in the semifinals. In 2003, we came back to beat SouthLake. 2004, Gary took them back to quarterfinals. In 2005, Katy was back in the championship again."

Listening to Coach Johnston, I realized that he has accomplished more in his lifetime than many ever dream about. Coach Johnston's leadership has been one of example, not one of talking about what needs to be done. I also saw an interesting parallel between his coaching era and that of Coach Brown before him. Both were concerned with the school's commitment to change. Seemingly, they both recognized that winning started at the head and filtered down through the body.

"Going back to my background, growing up in Galena Park at the time, you saw all those teams doing well. As a kid, I grew up dreaming of the day of being a Galena Park Yellow Jacket. Well, this is the same attitude today in Katy: the kids dream of someday being a Katy Tiger. There is a lot to that. I remember being in high school; what a thrill that it was walking through the dressing room! Walking outside into the stadium and looking up and seeing the place packed with fans. This was the thing to do in Galena Park on Friday and Saturday nights. Basically, when the Katy Tigers played at Rhodes Stadium, it was the same type of environment.

"When you factor in the playoffs, well, everybody loves the playoffs because the playoffs are the best games. It's a 'win or go home' situation. For some reason, this is when Katy Tigers are at their best.

"I think when I came here back in 1980, I knew the background out here. Mostly rice farmers, rural area, hard working folks; the gas plant was out here. You had a hard working class of people. I knew that that was a good foundation to build on. I'm not being judgmental when I say this, but the kids were not very mature."

"What do you mean Coach," I asked.

"Well they were not mature in the sense that they truly did not understand what it took to win. What happened, in my opinion, was the area started growing so fast out here, [with] Katy being the farthest 5A school [to the west]. Katy ISD started to grow back in towards the Houston area. Today, Katy ISD goes almost up to Dairy Ashford Road. So the east end of the district was growing rapidly. It was rough sledding out here in those days. I think that Gary will tell you, because he was here for the beginning of all this as well."

"Coach, what do you recall was your biggest challenge back then?"

"Well, the biggest challenge that I saw was the kids had no confidence. I mean none at all. I don't mean that in a bad way. Most of that was because they were getting beat from grade seven to twelve. I had people in the community telling me that our kids in Katy are more inclined to play basketball and baseball. I had to stop them right there and say I don't agree with them. I would say that it's just a matter of having more structure and some discipline. At first, they were taken back a little. But, through our efforts here, they saw that we truly wanted to show the kids that we knew just what it took to play the game of football.

"See I had been a coaching for some ten or eleven years back then, and I felt that at least I had a good understanding of what it took to get the kids mature enough to play the game. The first thing that we had to do was to get our kids into the weight room. Before we could do that, however, we had to get a weight room. You see, we didn't even have a weight room when I came in here. We had some weights out in the hallways. One varsity weight machine stuck in the wall. Again, that's one of those things that [happened because] the district was growing so fast, but we were not growing athletically.

"There, was just no budget there for us. There were no stipends for our coaches. In fact, our old field house was built back when Katy was a double A program. We had four different programs working out of that one little field house. Football, baseball, track here, and then we added soccer. We had only about one hundred and fifty athletes. They finally added a slab back here and then a weight room, back in 1985. Well, that was five years after I arrived here.

"So, it was a long time before we got a weight room. So we were simply not physically strong enough to play the game, in my opinion. We did not have the attitude or maturity to play 5A ball. Really, we had one key asset back then: We had good kids. But because they lacked confidence, they played hard until something bad happened. If you don't have faith, you simply fall at the first sign of adversity. That's why I say that we simply didn't have anything there. Just like the world, our kids needed to learn how to attack life after being presented with adversity.

"When I took over, I realized that we needed confidence and not in just football. We were getting killed in just about every sport but volleyball. We were on our fourth coach in about five years. Jack Rhodes, Sam Shields, and Bill came in, then me.

"We were on shaky ground when it came to football. Bill Haskett was our Principal back then. Again, I know that I have said this, I must say this again, If you are to give anybody any credit for turning Katy football program around, you have to start with Bill Haskett.

"Bill Haskett was the kind of Principal that you came in at the end of the year, sat down, and talked with him. His attitude was not one of criticizing. Bill always would ask you, 'What can we do to make it better?' He took the responsibility for what we were doing personally. So, if you want to know what the foundation of Katy football is built upon, I have two words for you - Bill Haskett. He would do everything possible to make it happen. I can honestly say that it was a joy to be head coach under Bill.

"See, I don't know if you knew it, but Bill grew up here! He was in the band in 1959 when they won State Championship. He saw how this community came alive by the events of 1959. So, he knew the importance of a successful athletic program, particularly in football. Now, back to what I was saying earlier, I asked Bill and Jack Rhodes, 'Are we going to do this the right way? Are we going to build a base, or are we going to bite the bullet?' I don't know if they really understood what I was asking at the time.

"Seeing that there was now confidence in the kids, I purposely kept all my freshmen players together. They went 5-5 that year. Before then, we had to use freshmen to help us fill the junior varsity and sophomore teams. Remember now, we only had 92-93 kids in the whole program.

"Our varsity was 2-8 that year. In 1983, I kept them all together again on the sophomore level. This was in an effort to help build their confidence. That sophomore team was 9-1, while our varsity was 1-9. Our sophomore kids were beginning to get excited about themselves. They were starting to feel like that could win State when they were seniors. In 1984, I kept all the juniors together except ten. Those ten were obviously the best ten in their positions, so they were moved up to varsity. That junior team was 8-2 that year, while the varsity went 1-9 again.

"In 1985, our varsity team was 4-6 that year. However, what most didn't understand was that those six losses that we had [were] by a combined total of 17 points. Other words, we were finally getting to be competitive. The next year in 1986, we went 10-0. I was starting feel that something special was happening here"

An aspect I noticed about Coach Johnston was that he still had a part of his heart in Katy football. I could see it in his eyes as he spoke about the past. "Coach, you don't hear a lot about Katy players that go on having big college or professional careers. But I have found that Katy has kids of great character coming out of the walls."

"Our whole deal was to build on the philosophy...I have always emphasized the character aspect over the athletic. This goes back to my philosophy about athletics, I tell everybody this. We spoke of being blessed. I feel blessed to be a head coach. I'm blessed to understand that God gave us a great tool in athletics, in particular, football. These young boys grow up to be young men that God wants them to be.

"As a Christian, we understand He molds and makes us when we get outside of our comfort zone. As long as we stay in our comfort zone, we are not going to grow. That's why we have that quote outside above the trophy case. 'When Excellence becomes Tradition, Greatness has no limits.' When you move outside your comfort zone, you do have an opportunity to experience greatness."

I had seen and heard that quote a number of times in Katy. To hear it from Coach Johnston's mouth made it come to life for me.

"Everybody wants to experience greatness, but do they have the courage to move outside their comfort zone to really find what it takes? I was talking earlier about having maturity. The mature athlete understands that they must find a way to get outside their comfort zone. If they are intimidated by pain, they are in the wrong sport. You need to go do something else. In football, you have pain every day. If you are intimidated by pain, you have to find something less demanding. I can't say that football is the greatest sport, but it is that most demanding sport.

"A good athlete is not discouraged by discomfort, pain, or inconveniences. Those things help to create a mature athlete to me. This is one of the underlying elements when you talk about the Katy tradition. Like I said earlier, you are going get hit, you're going to make some good hits. If you are a mature athlete, you will understand that, hey, the other team is here to play as well. You are going to have some good games and some bad ones.

"One of the things that I have always said, when the other team makes big plays, how you respond is what ultimately creates great character. Kids must learn to have respect for their opponent. You have to understand that you might lose a battle, but the objective is to win the war. You have to find a way to stay focused on those things. These are the things that don't happen overnight. They are the things that go back to being competitive and having maturity.

"That's why I say that it was such a process for us to develop the right mind set about what it takes to play this game. This is a great game. God gave me this great game to be a part of as an athlete and as a coach. This is a great thrill for me. When I say that I have been blessed, I mean it that I have been totally blessed.

Then, Coach Johnston's face took on a look of earnestness. I knew that he was passionate about what he was feeling. He was passing knowledge that he had wanted to share with the world for a long time now, knowledge that would help equip all of us with an understanding which would help get us through challenging times in life. I sat there listening appreciatively. This is what I wanted to uncover, the secrets of the countless spirits that made up KatyNation.

"I get up every day and pray. I pray that God uses me. I ask Him to bless what I do, to bless my coaches and our kids, and especially our schools. I love having the chance to tell people that I am one of the most blessed guys to walk on the face of the earth. When I arrived here back in 1980, I felt that this was the kind of community that would get behind us. In fact, in those first four years that I was the head coach, the time that we were getting our heads beat in, I was surprised, pleasantly surprised, when I looked up there and saw the big crowds at Rhodes Stadium. I thought, 'Lord if we could ever turn the corner and start to winning some games.' I could only imagine what the turnout would be like…."

"Coach Johnston, let me ask you this question. I would like to get your opinion on this. A lot of teams have the foundation of Christ in them. What sets Katy apart from the others? It seems like Katy has more fervor to me."

"Well, that's easy. It comes from the community that puts action to their belief. Another thing that helps Katy is that because the program is so special, sometimes a coach can get through to a competitive athlete better than a mom or dad can. For me, if I can make it something meaningful or a more personal experience for a kid, rather than something which will help us win a ball game or help us win a championship…those are the seeds that I was hoping for.

"This community has been lucky not only to have good coaches here but they also have good Christian men of faith. I know while I was here I had the kind of coaches that didn't just understand the game of football, the x's and o's, but they had the kind of goodness that would help them guide and direct these kids.

"A great example of this was 2002. We played Hastings in our own back yard. We got beat 14-13. It was the first district game that we lost in eight years. Then, [we] turned around and got beat by Elsik the last game of the year. We wound up being the third place team in our district that year.

"Now that was unheard of for the Tigers at the time. So, going in to the playoffs, we found ourselves playing Hastings again in the quarterfinals. I tried then to use this as a great opportunity to witness to our kids through athletics. 'Guys, we got beat by Hastings. In reality, we were fortunate that it was only 14-13; they outplayed us, and the score could have been greater.' I said to them that we went out there and tried to compete with them on our own strength. I tried to encourage that group: 'This is a great opportunity for you to pray to God for His strength to come through you and through your performance to make a difference.' We went out there and won 30-0, the same team that beat us 14-13 eight weeks earlier....

"I just hope that some of those kids will benefit from that throughout their lives. I realize that we are just a microscopic part of life's big picture. I hope that for some of those boys, when they run into difficult times, that they remember that game. You have to learn that when you have the Holy Spirit in you, and you are called to do something, that there is no need to doubt. Just go out and do it! I always hoped that the teams I coached and the coaches working with me will always have that kind of assurance and confidence. You just have to play to win and coach to win.

"Again, that's why I start out my morning with my devotion. I learned early not to ever let situations or circumstances rob you of your joy of being a competitive athlete. There's going to be a lot of adversity."

"That's amazing that you said that, Coach, because that has been my philosophy for about the last ten years: 'Don't let anything steal my joy.' No matter what my situation is."

Coach Johnston looked at me and smiled. He said, "That's a great philosophy to have. Adversities are always with us. I go back to 1985. I was feeling pretty good about the fact that we were 4-6. I had been called by my AD. He said, 'Coach, you might want to start looking.' I said, 'Look, I am a ball coach. I understand the scoreboard, and I know what they want. That's how it's been and that how it will always be.' Hey, we had our teeth cut on 5A ball. We were bloody every night. I knew in my heart if they would be patient and we could turn that corner, that we were so close. I told my boss that if we don't have a winning season next year, you won't have to ask me this again. I'll be glad to move on down the road. But, I believed in what we were doing and the way that we were doing it.

"Ever since then we have not had a losing season. In 1986, the kids went 10-0. In 1987, we were 5-5. 1989, we were 11-1, with our first playoff game. It was the best time that we ever had at that time. After that, we never missed a playoff. Every team is different because the leadership within. Senior leaders make the biggest difference with teams. With the '87, '90, and '01 groups, we had to face that arrogant pride, like everything else when you have a certain amount of success. The thing that you have to guard against is that arrogant pride....

"When I came here in the '80s, the kids were not committed. By that, I mean they were not willing to put in the extra time, only the minimum time that was required. Don't get me wrong; they were great kids. But, if you are going to compete to be a champion, you have to be willing to work for it. If you have to beg a guy to work, well it's going to be a while. Hard work has just got to be something in them.

"I think that I had it because my dad was a perfectionist; he was a pusher, no doubt about it. He could do anything. He was a carpenter, electrician; he did these things all very well. My two sons are like that. They are like my dad; he had an incredible mind. He could dissect and put things back together. I just don't have that gift. On the other side, I had a mother who was nurturing and supportive. So I was blessed to have this as a part of my background.

Factor in the community background that I grew up in, which took great pride in their high school football team. That's why I like coaching. I want all the kids that I coach to experience the success and feeling that I grew up with. I want it to be, maybe, one of the top ten experiences in their lives so that they can always reflect back on their high school career."

He stopped for a moment to take a sip of coffee. (I think that Coach Johnston was working on his fifth cup by this time.) "I truly understand what you are saying, Coach," I said. "I never really knew my father. In fact I just met him for the first time a few years back. But for me, it was the coaches along the way who helped give me that element of guidance and direction that all kids need. The role of a coach is truly an anointed role in a kid's lifetime. I think that the parent often takes that a little for granted. I will always cherish having that male figure in my life, a figure that came in many different sizes and shapes, many different personalities - both good and bad. To this day, I believe that being a coach is one of the greatest gifts that God has ever presented us."

The smile on Coach's face lit up like a light bulb. Then

he spoke again. "Well you have to understand what it takes to be a champion and compete on a higher level, like Gary Joseph. He understands that, and a lot of the other coaches here at Katy understand that. Let me say this, I am thankful that I have a wife that understands that. The years and time that it takes to build a championship program is very demanding. I never tried to abuse time. I never worked on Sunday morning. I could not expect God to bless what I am doing if I don't honor Him on Sunday mornings.

"We do spend time here. There is so much evaluation that is needed in a championship program, so you simply have to have your coaches putting in the time. We spend hours and hours just reevaluating our program and what we did through the year.... If you are going to stay out front, you have to find ways to continue to grow. We spend a lot of time doing our homework, evaluating everything that we did, so that when we got to spring training, we would have an idea of what we were going to do different, scheme-wise. Ideas for our offense, defense, or kicking game...all those types of things you have to address.

"I have coaches that have been asked to go and speak at different clinics, and they ask me, 'Well, what to you what me to tell them?' I say, 'Well, tell them the truth; we don't want to deceive coaches. The only way that they will learn is it you tell them the truth. If they are smart, they will find enough videotapes on the Katy Tigers out there, they are going to have what we are doing sooner or later. So, go tell them.' The thing is that we want to continue to grow. To me it's the same thing in the Christian walk; you have to continue to grow.

"In all, there are so many parallels in being a Christian and being a competitive athlete. Just coaching - I think that there are so many parallels there. Like I said a while ago, I have been more blessed than I deserve"

I was taken aback by Coach Johnston's candor. "Coach, you have a very humble spirit, and I'm sure that this, too, is a part of the equation for your success."

"Well, thank you, but I hope I never get to the point that I think I have all the answers. I just know the things that work for me. I don't respond to Mike Johnston's wisdom, I just think that God has blessed me with great insight. Thankfully, many of the coaches that I have been around over the years have picked up on it, and I hope that some of the kids that have played for us have picked up on it. There is no doubt that there are some things here that will help them compete in the real world, there's no doubt in my mind about that.

"One of the things that our coaches on Saturday morning would talk to the kids about is that there will come a time when these young boys will grow into young men and the fact they will have to learn how to experience putting somebody before yourself. [The coaches were] teaching [the boys] the importance of putting the team before themselves telling them that in life if you don't learn how to put your wife before yourself, then you are never going to be a very good husband; if you don't learn how to put your children before yourself, then you are never going to be a good father.

"Now, what better place can you practice this at this time in your life than being part of a football team, when you put your team before yourself? When you learn to put your team before yourself, you learn that you have a perfect opportunity to get rid of that pride and arrogance which can sometime be a by-product of being a winner...."

Sensing that we would be wrapping things up, I said, "Coach this has truly been helpful to me to be able to sit down with you to hear your thoughts about football and the

184

community of Katy."

"Oh good! I was hoping that I could give you enough to help you move forward with your project. I have been coaching for twenty-four years. Twenty-two years as the head coach and twenty-four total."

"So, Coach, you won three of the state titles here at Katy?"

"Yes, Gordon Brown won the first. Like I said, he was one of my college coaches. I have to say that he really made an impression on me. He is a good Christian man and strong in values. Some of the players that Gordon coached back in '59, [their] kids played for us here at Katy as well. "Today, Gary is coaching some of the sons of players that we had back in the '80s."

"Coach, do you ever see similarities from players that you coached and their kids who come along and play?"

"Ha! Yeah, yeah you do. In fact there one that is a sophomore here. His dad played for us in the early 80; his dad was very fast, and this kid runs real well. He has the speed like his dad had.

"The funny thing I was told long time ago [is] that if you want to project what kind of a athlete that a kid is going to be when he grows up, don't look at the dad, look at the mother. Two reasons: one their athletic talent, and second, you want to look at what kind of competitive spirit that she has. I want to tell you something, never was a truer statement ever made. In fact, I just recently had my Captains' Mother Meeting last Friday. It lasted three and a half hours!"

"Oh my goodness!" I said.

"We were getting ready for a parent meeting on Friday. Man, all you had to do was sit there, visiting those four women for a while, and you say, 'Well, I know why my captains are wired up the way they are.'"

185

Laughing out loud at what Coach had just said, I asked him if that saying were really true. "Hey, can't say a hundred percent, but it has just been my experience as a head coach. What I was told many years ago was so true. I mean, obviously, there are some that you look at the dad. I mean like Kevin Winslow, and you look at his dad. But that was the wisdom from Gordon Wood from many years ago. He had more wins than any other coach in the state of Texas at that time from Brownwood. I think that they won about seven state championships. It was a thrill for me to watch him and his coaching staff work the sidelines back at that time."

As Coach Johnston continued, when he spoke of something from his past that he liked or admired, he had this little twinkle in his eyes as he spoke about that particular situation. I told him that I had a chance to meet Bear Bryant once. Since we were sharing old war stories, I could relate to just what he was talking about. I told him that it was on the football field of Hofstra University back in 1981. I was a free agent wide receiver trying to make the squad with the New York Jets organization. One day at practice I had just lined up on the ball, and all of a sudden, players and coaches went sprinting over to the gate as if there were a fire drill.

Well, when all the smoke had cleared, it turned out to be Joe Willie Namath and Coach Bear Bryant. Thus, I could relate to how Coach Johnston felt about watching Gordon Wood in action. Though I had only heard Wood's name a couple of times, I knew that it was embedded in the hallowed grounds of Texas football.

Late in my interview with Coach Johnston, I brought up another story that I had heard. This story was one that only those in Katy really could have known. I knew that it was the kind of story that Hollywood movies were made of. It was a sensitive story, so I wanted to give Coach a chance to unwind and open up to me about his life first.

I wanted Coach Johnston to share this story so that you, the reader, could be aware of the kind of a man that he truly is. "Coach Johnston," I said, "I heard that there is another true story about you and a player by the name of Jason DeBusk." At the mention of Jason's name, Johnston's demeanor changed drastically. It was such a radical change that I wondered if I had asked a question that was inappropriate. It was then that I realized the power of Coach's conviction and love for kids. I wished that I had had a video camera team behind me filming Coach Johnston's response.

"The Jason DeBusk Fight Heart Award. As a coach, you have kids that somehow manage to reach inside you and make you a better person. Jason was a good-sized kid; in the spring of his freshman year, he was a 6'3" 227 pound kid that was filled with heart. A straight-A student, his goal was to be a physician one day. In spring training of his freshman year, Jason had come in to see the trainer Harold Bennett and had complained about his knee being sore.

"Harold told me that he felt like there was something going on inside his knee, so we sent him over to the team doctor. Mark Bing x-rayed him saw the tumor and immediately sent Jason over to M.D. Anderson Hospital for tests. They found that it was cancer, and they did the surgery and the chemotherapy. They did all that stuff that you have to go through with cancer.

"Then the beginning of his junior year, he decided that he wanted to come back out and play. Well, he got all the releases needed by his doctors, so we all welcomed him back in the program.

"He had lost about twenty-seven pounds since his freshman year. I could tell that he was a different kid after the surgery, so I moved him out to play tight end so that he would not have to be in the heart of all the action with that knee. Well, he made the spring game. He played about six or seven plays in the spring game, and he was thrilled. He was an inspiration to the other kids on the team. In fact, Jason had so much charisma that M. D. Anderson used him as a poster child to go around and speak to parents and children who were battling cancer.

"The kid had such a positive personality. You could see that he affected everyone around him. Well, he made it through the spring and was about to start the summer program. It was about the time that we were getting ready to go to coaching school. So, he comes to talk to me right before his senior year. He said, 'Coach, I hope that you guys will do a little about your coaching uniforms this year.' 'Why, what's wrong with our uniforms?' I asked. 'Well, nothing's wrong with them, Coach, they just are a little outdated, that's all.'

"Anyway, he comes back up here a couple of days later, and he hands me these red suspenders. He said that these would make me look more like a head coach. He was a young man who was excited about what he had gone through and happy to be a part of the program again. I was truly happy to see him smiling again.

"About three weeks later he comes back in and says, 'Coach, I don't think that I'm going to be able to play.' I looked at him, and I knew what he was trying to tell me. I just didn't want to hear him saying it. This kid was such a good kid, such a fighter. He was such an encourager to the rest of the kids. He had such a determination about himself to whip this thing."

Back in L.A., I often found myself on different movie sets, watching very talented actors perform. The actors and actresses are well trained. However, what most people never see is that those perfect scenes frequently require six to ten "takes" in order to make them seem real. As Coach Johnston shared this story with me, I could see that he was trying to fight off the great emotions. While he did a good job of holding back those emotions, the glaze in his eyes told me that he still carried the remnants of a broken heart.

He was not an actor; there was no supporting cast. But, if I could have found a way to present that scene to the world, it would have been worthy of Hollywood's finest awards.

"Jason followed the team around that year. He was a walking inspiration to all of us. I had a chance to see that, no matter what was going on in our lives, we had so much to be thankful for and no real reason to complain. When the team would walk up the ramp to the dressing rooms at game times at the stadium, he would always stay behind and wait for me, and we would walk up the ramp together.

"I never realized how much that it took for him to walk up that ramp each time. As we would get to the top, I could hear it in his breathing. I always asked him to come inside. But he never wanted his teammates to see him that that way. He would just wait out on the curb until we came out to start the game. Walking down the ramp was much easier for him.

"Anyway, we went through the season. He was one of our greatest cheerleaders that year. We beat Madison in the playoffs, and then we lost the next round. He got through to graduate, got a standing ovation. He had such a spirit of never, never, never giving up. In August, his cancer started to move aggressively throughout his entire body. We lost him the end of that summer.

"It was the spirit of never, ever giving up that seemed to follow us. There were many times that we would come from behind to win close games. We just believed that we were there to win. Like I said, we renamed the Fighting Heart Award to the Jason DeBusk Fighting Heart Award. From 1989 to 2003 when I retired, I put on those suspenders. Coach Bruno would always attach them for me in the back every game. He and I were very close to him.

"What an inspiration this kid was. He never made a tackle or caught a pass, but what an inspiration this kid was. This story will always be a special part of my career at Katy. Somehow that spirit has filtered down and found itself into a part of Katy's football program."

"Coach Johnston, I had heard pieces of this story, and it was very special to be able to hear it from you. I want to thank you for sharing it with me."

"Well as time as moved on, many sports writers and coaches came up to me and asked, 'Coach, what makes Katy so special? How does Katy do it?' I used to start out telling them that there is a special spirit in this community, a spirit of never giving up. Well, they would always go to another question when I would talk about the spirit. They seemed not to be able to digest the spiritual aspect of life. So, I decided to drop the spirit and leave the 'It.' So, every time they would ask me, I would reply, 'Katy has "It."' They would say, 'Well, what do you mean, Katy has "It"?' I would tell them that we have dedicated kids that really work hard. We have a great staff; we have a good program, and we have great administrative support. We have a great band, cheerleaders, and drill team. We have great student support and great community support. Just whatever 'It' is, we have 'It'! 'It' is a special thing.

Handing me a copy of a program that resembled a small town's yellow page book, he said, "Look at this Dexter. I see that they are using 'It' as a part of the Katy slogans today on their football programs." I smiled when saw the "It" on the front cover of the program. "So most people don't know that the 'It' is an abbreviated form of SPIRIT, do they?

Looking at me like a proud father, he smiled and nodded his head twice. "That's what 'It' is. 'It' is a great spirit!"

Driving back to Houston that evening after having dinner, I considered that I had interviewed a very special person. I thought about what Coach Johnston reminded me of when I called him and Coach Joseph "legends" when I first met him. It was a quote from the Houston Oilers' Coach Bum Phillips: "The only good legend is a dead one." I knew that Coach Phillips was wrong, because I had just spent the afternoon with a live one.

Walking in Front of the Shadows

Coach Gary Joseph

Most people who find themselves following in the footsteps of those who have been successful before them, often find themselves walking in the shadows of greatness, faced with the challenge of trying to live up to those before them. This is not the case with Coach Gary Joseph. Somehow, life has found a way to place him in front of the greatness that once came before him, which creates a very unique situation.

My next book *KatyNation2* will cover the current characters of the Katy football program. It will look into the lives of coaches, players and boosters who continue to work hard, carrying the torch of tradition that those in the community demand to see burning before them. I feel, however, that I must introduce to you in this book the person responsible for keeping that flame alive.

To those in the football community, Gary Joseph is more like the governor than the head football coach. The loyalty by which this community embraces him is no accident. The passion in their eyes when they speak of him goes far beyond human understanding. The responsibility that this individual must carry on his shoulders cannot be found through his quiet and soft-spoken demeanor.

However, as the voices of time still echo in my mind,

I better understand what the responsibility of Coach Joseph details. I assure you that he has been walking in the footsteps of giants and is leaving even larger imprints behind. I knew when I started this journey that Coach Joseph was the head of a very special high school football program. What I didn't understand, however, was how he found himself at the helm of such a powerful machine. While researching and studying the history of Katy's football program, it became increasingly clear that Coach Joseph had been predestined for this role.

My follow-up call to Coach Joseph came in around Wednesday of that week. I introduced myself and tried to give him a better understanding of the project that I was undertaking. He said, "I look forward to meeting you. How about ten o'clock tomorrow?"

Walking into the big red doors of the field house where Coach Joseph's office was located, I saw a huge glass trophy case adorning an entire wall. At first, one would think that you were at a business that sold trophies to the public, until you looked closer and saw that the countless trophies in the case had been engraved with 'Katy High School.'

Behind the wall, I could see a state-of-the-art weight training facility. There was no doubt that I had found myself in the den of champions and at the beginning of a very special journey. Above the trophy case, I saw for the first time the quote "When excellence becomes tradition, greatness has no limits." It was a quote that would follow me forward.

Coach Joseph's office was on the left when I walked inside. I could see his secretary working through the glass window in the door. Opening the door, I introduced myself. She introduced herself as Connie. She told me that Coach was not in, that he had stepped out for just a moment. Sitting there, I shared with Connie my purpose for visiting with Coach Joseph. She instantly became excited. Apparently,

Connie had a son who was once a part of the Tiger program. She shared a few Tiger stories with me. The one thing the Katy community was not short on was Tiger stories!

In the room, it was difficult to find a bare spot on the walls. They were filled with awards and plaques that commemorated the successful heritage of Katy's football program. It felt like a shrine rather than a secretary's office. Then Coach Joseph came in the office, wearing his "patient coach's hat." It's part cowboy hat, part "Yes, I can take you on the golf course hat."

"Hey, Dexter, it is a pleasure to meet you; come on inside. Have a seat, can I get you anything."

"No thanks, Coach, I'm fine."

"So tell me about this project. This book that you are writing." I began to explain to him how I had stumbled across the remarkable story behind the success of the Katy High School football program and that I was at the point of the passing of the torch to him and his staff.

I had presented myself so many times to my research subjects, by the time that I made it to Coach Joseph, I didn't realize how naturally those words seemed to simply roll off my tongue. A part of me was a little saddened that I had come to this point into the book. Even though I still had the screenplay and the book *KatyNation2* to write, I still regretted ending this one. I sat there across Coach Joseph's desk, wondering what words that he might share with me to help me complete this portion of the project.

Taking out my little tape recorder, I smiled to myself. It was something that I did subconsciously by now, knowing that again I was pressing that travel button back into time. Placing the recorder on Coach's desk, I was prepared to take the journey again.

"Coach, this is a remarkable program. How did it all

get started for you?"

"Well, let's see now, I have to go back to 1982 when I came in as the secondary coach. I was the coordinator over in Westlake out of Austin, Texas before I came here."

"Coach Joseph, were you raised in Austin?"

"No, I was raised in Wharton. My dad was the coach of Wharton High School. He actually coached me there. My dad moved to Westlake my second year in Austin. He became the head of the high school coaches' association. I had a chance to coach my brother there at Westlake."

"Oh, wow, that had to be a unique situation. You hear of dads coaching their sons but not of brothers coaching their brothers."

"It was a tough decision coming here. I had a pretty good job in Westlake. I was the defensive coordinator there."

"What made it such a tough decision Coach?"

"Coming here was one of those things; Katy had become a 5A school and was taking a pounding at the time. I didn't really didn't know much about their history when I first got here. I really didn't know what chance that we had in turning the program around. The fact that I was raising a family at the time...I had to factor that into my decision of making my move here."

"So soon, I moved here. I knew that I had made the right decision. The people here were not pretentious. They were the kind of folks that would talk to you and share their thoughts, both good and bad about the program. The first couple of years here were tough. We lost so bad in the early '80s that it was tough to take at times. I knew that about coaching; nobody wants to face it. And it's not an enjoyable thing to have to go though; losing is always a difficult thing, and the coaches are the first to not enjoy it.

"For most programs, it is a make-you or break-you

situation. I believe that we coached as hard back when we were 1-9 as we did when we were 10-0. It was quite obvious that we were not used to winning back then, and we lost a lot of games because of that.

"Except for the 1959 team, the tradition has not always been as deep as it is today. When we started winning, it became expectation, and we started to build confidence."
"Coach Joseph, how did you get through those times? I remember in my interview with Coach Johnston that he said that his back was truly up against the wall to the point many were demanding his head. How did you handle it?"

"It was tough; it was tough on you and tough on your family. In my opinion, what got us through was the fact that we still had great kids. We had kids that would let you coach them. As the first group from the earlier 80s started to turn the corner, we began to see their confidence change as well as the desire to become competitive. A few wins can go a long way with a kid.

"It was important for us to see a group of kids complete the cycle. This would give us a chance to see a more complete assessment of what our program was going to look like in the future. After that, we didn't have to keep the kids together to establish anything. After the first cycle of kids, we could begin to bring kids up to face the stronger competition. The kids know to expect a win, not just their class, but throughout the program.

"The group that I have today, they were 2-8 and 1-9. But, as juniors and seniors, they expect to win. When I was talking to them last spring, they were afraid of screwing up. They were afraid of screwing up the tradition and letting everybody down."

"Coach, how did you pick up on that?"
"Well, I began to sense it through our meetings, and

when a kid wants to be a captain and take on leadership roles, I become aware of his beliefs."

"In a way, Coach, that is quite a compliment. In essence, they were paying a huge compliment to the program. They were indirectly saying how much they respect and cherish the program that you have help to create."

"Yes it was, but even if we were not in the spot that we are right now, I told them that you can't worry about something that you have no control over. Yes, the tradition is a part of it, and our expectations are of it. The only thing that you can do is to do your best. I am thankful that we have done as well as we have, because the seniors that we have now, these kids believe that there is always a chance…that if they work hard enough they still have an opportunity to do something. They always have the hope that they can win. From that perspective, it's been good.

"Even today we still have our challenges, and I'm sure that most people don't realize what we have to go through to continue to win. Some do, but most have no idea."

"Coach Joseph, what do you think has been your biggest challenge since you have been here?"

"I think helping them to learn how to win has been our biggest challenge. Winning, and being constant at it, is always a challenge for coaches. Being on the outskirts of Houston, we still try hard to maintain the high integrity of the program that has been established.

"We are not naive enough to think that we have done a lot of things different. But, we still hold our kids accountable here. There are some principles that we believe in; they [students] are not going to drink and smoke. Anybody stealing is gone. We still have high moral values here. We are still an old-fashioned community. I think that this is probably another one of our biggest challenges.

"Houston is growing right out here. I've been here twenty-two years, and I have seen it all come out this way. Even though Katy has expanded as well, you just don't want your kids to get caught up in that kind of a lifestyle."

"One of the questions that I wanted to ask you is how do you go about finding coaches to complement what you are doing? What do you look for in coaches that separates them from just being mediocre to being great?"

Coach Joseph looked back at me with a smile on his face. "Well, many people get into this business for all the wrong reasons. You have to be here because you care for the kids. I listen carefully to those that I wish to bring aboard." In a quiet voice he said to me, "If they are constantly using the word 'I,' instead of 'we,' then a red flag goes up in my mind. I want people around me to express their opinions. That is very important to me. But when we walk out of the office, everyone has to be of the same opinion. It is important that we be of the same opinion, because kids can pick up on those kinds of things very easily. I have been fortunate to be around some great coaches."

"But, Coach, that could not have been a accident. Why is it that your path has taken on this direction? What was it that helped you to make the right choices?"

"I have to honestly go back to my dad. I had that foundation of underlying knowledge and understanding for the game. I knew what I was getting into when I got into coaching. I had been with him and watched him. Of course, my mother was a great coach's wife, and that's just as important as anything else that makes a good coach. We have a lot of coaches that come here as young kids. I would always tell them that it's not about quantity, it's about quality.

"I never felt cheated by the hours that my dad put into coaching. He always took care of us, and he always found a way to keep us involved, just like my coaches today. It is important that they understand what they do; they have ownership in this program. Coach Johnston used to tell us that we are not working for him, we are working with him. That's what we believe in around here.

"I hope that our coaches will tell you that it's not our program, but it's the community of Katy and the schools. When I first came here, we were not winning in anything, except volleyball, and that's it. Johnston created a new foundation for us, and Katy started winning in other sports, as well. The strange thing about winning is that it breeds an attitude for winning throughout the entire school and into the community. It was not always that way."

"What kept you from 'turning around and running' in those lean years, Coach?'

"I thought about it, I talked to some people, but it all came down to 'was it a better job than I have or was I more caught up in a title.' I thought about other possibilities after we had won State in 1997. I have to be honest; I was beginning to get antsy, but my kids were here. I wanted to see them through school at the time."

"Well, you just touched upon something that Coach Johnston mentioned about a good coach…he has to be willing to place others before himself. You just gave me an example of that, by what you just said about your kids. Putting your family before your own desires."

"It is important to understand that. We had a lot of coaches that have come through here. Putting in the hours and the time was just too much for them. There are a lot of coaches that put in more time that we do. Like I tell our coaches, 'We are going to work until our work gets done. Then you go home and be with your family.' It takes a lot of time, what we do here, but even more than that, it takes true commitment. Those victories that you see on Friday and Saturday come from coaches who have committed themselves.

"As far back as '85 and '86, I knew that I could not do my job without the support of those around me. You have to have good coaches."

"Coach Joseph, what makes you so consistent in your approach to football?"

"I think that there is no doubt your background and upbringing helps to create consistency. We were taught hard work. To be honest with you, I grew up as a coach's kid; we didn't have a whole lot. We had to work for what we got.

"I always wanted an opportunity to coach kids, I knew that if I was going to do that, I wanted to do my best. I think that some of these things are the underlying elements to being consistent. You add in the countless quality relationships with the kids along the way that we encounter. It makes this thing fun."

"Coach, were you around with when Jason," and before I could say another word,

"Debusk."

"Was that tough on the team?"

"It was tough on Coach Johnston. The program was able to get through it. It was really tough on Coach, because Coach was really close with the kid. When he moved him to tight end, Mike was around him every day and all the time. Just like everyone in your program; you become a part of them, and these kids become a part of your heart. Part of your job as a coach is to help a kid overcome their handicap, whatever that is.

"Mike felt like with Jason, that we could get him to fight through this. The kid was so articulate that it made him even more special. He spoke with so much courage and conviction that it was not before long he had everyone pulling for him. The fact that Coach had no control over the situation seemed to pull him deeper into it. Coach believed that you could change those things that you had control over. This thing, however, was different. I think that the worse off Jason got, the more of an inspiration he became."

"What do you think that your biggest challenge is today as a coach?"

"Right now, I think that it is the fact that I don't want to see the quality of this program go down. The make up of any school changes with time. Trying to maintain the heritage and consistency of the community which is constantly changing is a challenge. There have been a lot of people who have worked countless hours for this program to get this far. Names and faces that are sometimes lost over the years. But this is their legacy that I am overseeing today.

"Of course, I welcome the challenge, but like Coach Mike was saying, it is easier to handle the things that you can control. It's those things that are out of your control that increase that challenge. This is such a special community. I like having a chance to coach kids whose parents I coached years ago. So when you talk about Katy having a great heritage, it is more than what lies on the surface. If Katy High ever loses that sense of community, then I think that we will be like every other school.

"The one thing that we have here which separates us from most is that we still have that small-town community. Even though we are growing in size, we still have that feel of a small town which still cares for one another.

"One thing that I can said about Katy, and Mike will confirm this, that one of the things that we have been blessed with is that the parents here have allowed us to coach these kids."

"How much a part of winning is that, Coach?"

"It is a very big part of it. A lot of parents and people feel like they are supposed to have a say in the coaching part of it. This creates the political atmosphere that, quite frankly, takes you away from coaching your best. Here, once we started winning, people started to feel like the coaches knew what we were doing.

"Our kids here are not afraid to work hard. They believe in the tradition that comes with this program. From elementary to 'Pop Warner' football, they look forward to being a part of this Katy Tiger program someday. That is a great thing to have, kids that truly don't mind working hard towards excellence."

"Coach you just reminded me of something that I just saw the other night on television. A sportscaster was interviewing the head football coach over at Madison High School. The one thing that stood out in my mind was when he said that kids today do like to work hard. He said that today's kids do put forth the effort to do what it takes to get the job done. This was the same coach that worked with the ex-Texas quarterback Vince Young."

"That's one thing that we have here at Katy, the parents will allow us to work these kids. First of all, if the parents don't believe in what you are doing, it is just not going to work. If the kids go home and complain about practice, and the parents don't say, 'Everything will be all right,' then it just won't work. Now that we have been established, the parent can say, 'If you want to win, this is what you need to do.

"That's one of the things that we did not have early on. We had not proven that we could win and win on a consistent basis. Once we had won a championship, then we created the respect from the parents. Yes, we do know what we are doing. These things might seem small, but they are monumental in being consistent as a winner. We have won around here because they have been a team, kids who put others before themselves. That is something that is very hard to teach, especially when you have parents that are not willing to work with you as for as playing the best players, even if that means not playing their kids.

"That's been very important, because these parents and kids understand that they have to sacrifice sometimes for the good of the whole. That's a hard thing to do. It's hard to have a kid sit there and watch someone play before him. Whereas many kids from other schools today play for scholarships, our kids play to win championships. The only way to win championships is to be unselfish and to put other before you. People wonder what the difference is about Katy. We have kids that are willing to play for the betterment of the whole.

"The thing is that if you don't fit into a mold, you will not be a scholarship player in the first place. Here we have kids who are all a part of this program. We have teachers that keep us informed with a kid's progress, which makes [the teachers] a part of the program. Our teachers here are just as important as our coaches. They are the coaches in the classrooms. If our kids don't get it done in the classrooms, there is no chance that they can get it done here. There is so much to a winning program that on the outside many do not recognize.

"We have teachers that will email me and tell me if a kid is not getting it done, which helps us to catch any problems before it becomes to late. This is why winning here is such a community effort; everyone associated with this winning tradition contributes to the success of the program. If I find a kid that is not getting it done, we have a study period in the morning before school starts. We make them realize that they will have to get it done on their time if they don't get it done in the classroom. So, that means they have to get up earlier, get to school, and put in their time. They soon realize that it is easier to get it done in the classrooms.

"It's important for us to know if a kid is failing, but it's more important to know why he is failing as well. This helps us to make better adjustments and help them to get on the right track. We could not do this without our teachers' support. Our teachers' support enables us to go to the parents with greater information to help improve the situation. That's why it is so important to have great assistant coaches that are on top of their game as well. Everyone one plays a vital role in the winning tradition that many people read about."

"Could you imagine having the responsibility that you have today, back in 1959 when Coach Brown was coaching?" We both laughed.

"Yes, they only had thirty kids on the whole team. Today, we have thirty kids just in our secondary." Shaking his head, "We have about three hundred and thirty in our whole program today. We don't cut anybody in our football programs. That has been a good thing for us, and people don't understand. This is about a program; it's about a school; it's about a community; it's about being a team.

"We are trying to teach these kids that, when they leave school, at least they will learn how to sacrifice for somebody else. If I had to leave a message with this community, I would have to say, 'Don't ever lose respect for what they have here. Don't feel like they are not appreciated.' There is no doubt that this community is our greatest asset. The one thing I hope never happens here. I hope that Katy never turns into 'just another school.' I believe that Katy has been a place where people would want to raise their kids. The make up of this community has allowed us to be successful.

"As Katy continues to grow, and outsiders move this direction, I hope that they will understand the sacrifices that this community makes for this football program. I believe that this will help them to adjust and become an important part of this community. Growth is a wonderful thing. Learning to adapt to the structure of a winning program is always a concern for me. Those old-fashioned moral values are embedded into this community, and quite frankly, they work for us here. Finding a way not to lose those values is important for this community's survival. That Christian background that has been established for our kids. People want to know what makes us different. That is what I see which separates us from the most."

"I'm glad that you mentioned that, Coach. We live in a time where it is not politically correct to express the truth about Christianity. Throughout my research for this book, it is that factor that has become the one common denominator that has presented itself to me over and over again. The Spirit of Christ. Not in words but in action. Not in arrogance but in humble hearts.

"Even though the world might not want to hear it, that spirit is alive and well. For me to find it present in a whole community and watch it manifest itself throughout a high school football program has been a special gift for me. Coach, thank you for giving me this time."

"You are welcome Dexter."

"I want to end this book with the passing of the torch to you and your administration. In the next book, *KatyNation2*, I will dive into more of your philosophies, the coaches and players. I just thought that this book should pay homage to the history of the community and the coaches who paved the way."

Walking out of Coach Joseph's office, I honestly felt as I had spent time with a special human being. Greatness comes to us in so many different forms. But when we see it bottled up in an humbled spirit, filled with sacrifice and unconditional loyalty, it makes us understand what we all have a chance to become. Over twenty-five years in a program, and this man still walks before the shadows of those who came before him.

How he managed to embrace the patience to wait his turn to carry the torch of Tiger pride is something more challenging than anything that I have every encountered. To be disciplined enough to stay the course and not be distracted by his own desires is something that any political figure in this country can learn from. Coach Joseph's ability to lead through action and not through only words is a character trait that all of us can pursue.

In the passing weeks after my interview with Coach Joseph, I watched him from the sidelines of a number of Katy games. I wanted to get a closer view of him and his coaching staff for the next book. What I saw was very powerful.

I observed that opposing teams were not simply taking on the opposition. They were taking on the whole community of Katy. No matter whom Katy came up against, this was the force that they brought to each battle. If Texas A&M had the Twelfth Man, the Tigers had KatyNation behind them. This large sea of red and white spectators washes over the stands on game day, and they refuse to leave before they drown the opposing fans.

Whoever wrote that there was power in numbers must have come from Katy, Texas. These fans have been gathering since 1939 and carry with them the spirit of winning. Countless photographers have tried to capture the picture of this spirit. To fully appreciate it, you simply have to come to a Katy game and see "It" for yourself.

It is said that true leadership starts at the head. If that is the case, then Coach Joseph carries the torch of the spirit of Tigers very well. He has seen to it that the professionalism of his coaching staff strongly resembles that of a college program on game day. Behind the coaches, Coach Joseph has a tribe of gladiator-like warriors pacing the sidelines, waiting for a chance to step onto that sacred patch of green carpet one hundred yards long. Behind the mighty Tigers, completely caged off by a concrete barrier, is something like no other giant in the country. Roaring with sounds of hunger, this beast reaches over its restraints to devour the sparse number of fans of the opposing team. They are Katy; they are KatyNation.

Coaching Tiger Cubs

Coach Robert Turney

There are many different elements that make up a successful high school program. When the Katy Tigers take the field on Fridays and Saturdays, most fans forget about the fact that the huge Tigers running up and down the field were once little cubs who were barely able to move their own body weights before they arrived at Katy High School. They were once little athletes stumbling over blades of grass that covered the football field.

Today, fans scream and yell when they see #30, the extremely hard-nosed running back Aundre Dean break from the pack and show the opposing team what true power is all about. Fans stand to their feet when one of the Fuda brothers plucks the football in full stride as if he had huge vacuum cleaners attached to his hands, enabling him to suck balls out of the air like some bizarre super hero.

Most people forget that these young players got their start right here in the Katy Independent School District. In fact, Katy ISD boasts over twenty-seven elementary schools and ten junior high schools. Katy Junior High and West Memorial Junior High are the two schools that feed into the powerful high school of Katy.

One evening while I was walking the sidelines of a Katy game, I met a young man by the name of Clayton Odem. Mr. Odem was one of the assistant principals over at West Memorial Junior High. Later in my conversation with him, I found out that he used to coach at Katy High School.

He never mentioned it, but I later found out that Clayton was actually the first African-American football coach to coach at Katy High School. After he discovered that I was writing *KatyNation,* Clayton suggested that I come in to interview one of his coaches over at West Memorial named Robert Turney. He told me that "Coach Rob," as he called him, was a scout for Katy High back in the days of Coach Mike Johnston.

I always like to get two or three different perspectives of a person as I write about him, so I thought that a meeting with Coach Rob could possibly help me to better understand a little more about what really made Coach Johnston "tick." *KatyNation* is more than a book about a successful high school football program; it is also about the countless people who make up the Katy community.

A couple of months after I met Clayton, he introduced me to Coach Rob. When I met Mr. Rob, I knew that he was the kind of character with whom I would enjoy visiting. He had that "old school look," with the energy and excitement of a twenty-year-old. We scheduled a lunch and fed our stomachs over at a local barbecue place called Nonmachers on Mason Road. After we both ordered Nonmachers' famous sliced beef sandwich, we sat down at one of the little rustic tables and blasted back into the past.

"Dexter, one of the people that I want you to meet is a teacher over at West Memorial; her name is Teresa McMeans. Her father was one of the original rice farmers of Katy. He will be able to give you some great information about the history of Katy."

I smiled to myself, I had already interviewed Teresa's father. He was the same Melvin Jordon that you read about earlier in the book. It is truly a small world.

"I know of this guy, Coach; I had a wonderful time

interviewing him."

"Oh good. Well, Teresa married a guy named Garland McMeans whose father opened up West Memorial and later went on to open up Taylor High School"

"Coach Rob, when did you actually begin your career in Katy?"

"I arrived at West Memorial in 1977. I have been in that office for almost thirty years. I never coached at Katy, but most people do not realize that up until a few years ago, the junior high coaches were responsible for the scouting reports on other teams for Katy High School.

"You see, what we do when we coach the junior high kids is use the exact same terminology as the high school coaches...the exact plays that Katy Tigers use. We try and put the exact same style of youngster in the same positions that they would be in when they get over to Katy."

"How did this come about, Coach?"

"Mike Johnston! Mike had all the junior high coaches at West Memorial and Katy Junior High meet over at his office. He sat all the coaches down and he said 'We would do it this way. We will come out to watch you practice.' It all started with Mike.

"One of the things that many junior high teams try to do is to put a big kid who was meant to be a linemen in the back field and have him run over smaller kids to win games. But when that kid gets to the next level, he won't be a running back. He's going to be in that offensive line. So rather than put a big kid in a position that he would not play later, we made the sacrifice of winning games. We made the players play the positions for the next level.

"When Mike was there, and I am not sure whether they still do this or not, but the freshmen class offense got the first three picks of players. The kids that could catch were placed on offense, and the real aggressive kids that could run were placed on defense. Defense got the next eleven players because defense is very important to the Katy High School program."

"That's really interesting, Coach. The junior high school actually helps to create a Tiger connection. You guys are just as much of the high school program as the high school coaches. You have the responsibility of preparing these kids before they even get to the next level"

"Yes, we help to teach the kids the very basics. When they get to high school, the coaches add on to that. Have you had a chance to talk to coach Bruno yet?"

"No, I was going to wait to interview all the coaches for my next book, *KatyNation2*."

"Well, make sure that you talk with him. He was the linebacker coach and one of the best in the business at that. If you saw Mike Johnston going to a football game, Bruno was one right next to him.

"I hired on with Jack Rhodes when we were 3A. We were in the district with Huntsville, A&M Consolidated, and Brenham. Back then, Katy still had that 'small-town feeling,' still had that 'little community feeling.' Real friendly people would invite you to come over to their house for lunch. The community starting growing so fast that we could not build schools fast enough."

"What do you think attributed to the fact that the Katy district grew so fast?"

"I think that people wanted to get out away from the congestion of the city. Taylor became the second Katy High School. It was named after the superintendent back then. Let me tell you a story about Mr. Taylor. He would drive around at night, and if he saw a light on in one of the buildings, he would report it back to the coach the next day and let you know that this was not acceptable. He was known to be pretty tight with the district's money.

"Well that first year that I was with Jack Rhodes, Katy played all games on Friday nights. But the junior high coaches had to go out and scout the other schools' teams for Katy. We would come back on Saturday and give a scouting report. The deal with Jack was that all junior high coaches had to come up to school, not just the ones giving the report. We were like one big happy family. All coaches had to come in and listen to the report. When all that was said and done, we would have our junior high meeting. Jack wanted to know what he could do to improve our junior high program. So there was a tremendous amount of effort directed to our programs. This is where Katy High kids got their start.

"Nowadays, it's different, but back then when we were involved with the program, we followed the teams into the playoffs. I remembered going out to scout an Odessa Plano game. Odessa had ten thousand fans on one side of the stadium and another five thousand on the visiting Plano side. That's how big Texas football is.

"I worked with Jack Rhodes in my first year, and then Katy made him an offer. He could either remain as the Head Coach of Katy high or become the Athletic Director of both schools. Jack took the Athletic Director's job, which opened up two coaching jobs, one at Katy and one at Taylor. Jack's receiver coach at Katy, Lester Reinaker, went on to become the first Head Coach at Katy Taylor. So, Jack was at Katy from 1968 to 1977. He was the athletic director 1978 through 1985.

"We had to get a coach at Katy, so they brought in a guy named Sam Shields. Sam was with the group of coaches that came in who lived in the field house.

"Their homes in Jacksonville had not sold yet. They

did not have the money yet to buy their new homes, so they lived in the field house in June, July, and August. Sam's brother was the Offensive Line Coach Tom Shields. They slept in there; they ate in there; they showered in there; they shaved in there. We would be having meetings and alarm clocks would go off. Sam lasted one year. I think Katy was like 0-10 or 1-9, I can't remember.

"Sam was followed by a guy named Bill Byron. Bill had a successful program from Brownwood back in 1965. Bill's offensive line coach was a man by the name of Mike Johnston. Bill took a coaching job up around Dallas. Mike came over to the head job in 1980."

"So, what really turned the Katy Tiger program around, Coach?"

"No doubt, it was Mike Johnston. Mike brought in a winning spirit with him; it didn't happen overnight. Even on the junior high level, I remember one of the junior high coaches bringing a sub-par scouting report back to Mike. The coach said that one of the teams that we were about to play was on just an average football team. Mike pushed his chair back hard and said, 'There are no average teams in this division. This is 5A ball; I need a much better scouting report than that!'

"Mike demanded more out of everybody around him, even on the junior high level. As scouts, we looked at Katy's opponents as thoroughly as we could. What we gave to Coach Johnston would determine how well the team could be prepared. We presented oral reports and written reports for the high school coaching staff. Today, with the help of computers, it's done differently. But we used to be a major part of the program.

"When Mike came along, he was more demanding in the scouting reports. He wanted to know the other team's 'bread and butter' plays…what they ran on first downs, second downs, third downs. He wanted to know what was the other team's snap count, what they do on the goal line. He made us better at what we did. In turn, we actually became better junior high coaches.

"I'm sure that you heard that when Mike got there, the weight room was like a ghost town. He really didn't have much of anything at all to work with.

I'm sure that Coach Mike will tell you today that the majority of the success over there has to do with the off-season program. Once he got those kids to get committed to working in the off-season, that's when things began to change for the program. When the season was over, they would give them a couple of weeks off, and then the coaches would start their off-season program."

"Coach, has the community always been so supportive?"

"Yes, once we started winning, it was like a magnet. They really became glued to the program. Even the younger kids began to desire to become a Katy Tiger someday. The passion to become a part of the program seemed to grow wild."

Coach Turney had a great impersonation of Coach Johnston. He made me laugh every time he would say something that Coach Johnston used to say.

"I don't know if you have ever heard this before, but Coach Johnston had a daily routine that he was passionate about. Every morning, he would get up very early and get his coffee and then his Bible. He would read the scriptures, then, go take his jog and get showered. He would be at school for a 6:00 a.m. coaches' meeting. He was consistent: 3:00 a.m., Bible; 4:00, jog; 5:00, shower; and 6:00, coaches' meeting.

"A lot of his stories to the kids and coaches were scriptures from the Bible. He reminded everyone in the program that they had to submit; they had to sacrifice if they truly wanted to be a champion. Today, everyone is afraid to talk about the Word, but Mike would quote the scriptures; and he was not afraid to pass it on. Of course the way it is today, you cannot pray at school; you can't lead the kids in prayer. But Mike found a way to teach the kids things through the messages from the Bible."

Coach Turney continued in the voice of Coach Johnston, "'You know, we play Friday night. You will be up here early to stretch; I see you Saturday morning. You all know where you need to be on Sunday.' He didn't say, 'Go to church.' He said, 'You all know where you need to be on Sundays.'" We both laughed and smiled.

"On Wednesday night in the off season, he would be with the coaches and go over the different elements of the game. One night, it would be the special teams' breakdown; another night, something different. And you know what Wednesday night was, don't you."

I looked at him, and simultaneously we said, "Bible Study!"

"Most coaches would get up on Saturday morning and go play golf. Coach Mike would go find a good football game. Football was his job and his hobby at the same time.

"I know that I have told you this before. Katy won many, many football games when they had nowhere near the talent as a lot of the other teams. Many years, they would be ranked 8th or 9th in the city. They had no blue chippers, but they would always find a way to win. Now, you tell me if Coach's belief did not have something to do with that! The other schools would have two or three kids who had already committed to Texas or Texas A&M.

"We would line up head to head, and we would beat

them. So many times, the outside world would say, 'Katy's going to lose; Katy's going to lose.' But we would turn around and beat them. So many times we have pulled that off. Over half of playoff games were games, on paper, that we were not supposed to have won. The school just finds ways to win."

Coach Turney and I finished our lunch and headed back to his office. We talked about Katy football all the way back. Even though today Coach Turney coaches basketball over at West Memorial, I could still see his love for the Katy program of which he was once a part. The spirit of Katy football still lies in the hearts of those who where once a part of it. It is almost impossible to explain the true power and magnitude of such a program.

Each person whom I came to meet seemed to be so overwhelmed and excited about being a part of Katy's success. One fact clear to me was that if you found yourself somehow, at sometime, a part of the Katy's Tigers program, then it was a lifelong passion which would follow you forever.

A Family of Tigers

Blanche Fussell

The first time that I heard the name "Blanche Fussell" was early in my research. It was at my stop at the tourist center in Katy that I first heard the name. Later, Coach Gordon Brown mentioned the name several times. I always enjoy following leads that I uncover along the way. It is truly what makes writing so much fun. The first time that I saw Blanche was at her nephew's wake, although I didn't have a chance to meet her. I did meet her daughter Sandy and her son Dwayne. Dwayne was the quarterback who led the Tigers to their first state championship game back in 1959.

Sandy was kind enough to open the lines of communication between Blanche and me. I finally managed to schedule a time to embrace her thoughts on early life in Katy, Texas. I had no idea that my interview with her would be so rewarding. I had gathered information about early Katy primarily from men. I knew that if I wanted the real story, I had better get it from a woman's point of view. I am glad I did.

Still residing in the heartbeat of downtown Katy, Blanche was easy to find. After I rang the doorbell, a woman's voice from the other side of the door rang out, "Be right there."

"Okay," I replied.

Inside, Blanche greeted me. I was surprised by her strength. As a kid, I always thought of someone in her eighties as being old. Blanche had the energy of a fifty-year-old. Though her walk had slowed, her physical presence was

217

one that I thought was strong in body and spirit. "Thank you so much for taking the time to see me," I said.

Early in the interview, I had to smile to myself, because it was I who was being interviewed at first.

"What made you want to write a book about Katy football in the first place? Where are you from, who have you spoken with?"

The one thing that I have learned about most older people is that they are direct and to the point. I always found that refreshing. At least you knew where you stood with them.

I took the first fifteen minutes of our interview to present myself to her and tell her how this project got started. Soon, I felt that the interview was revolving around me rather than her. I was a stranger who had walked into her world, asking questions about her past. It would be on her time that I would be welcomed. There was a picture sitting by her chair. I assumed that Mr. Fussell was next to her in the photograph. When she picked it up and placed it in my hands, I knew that our interview had been elevated to that of two friends talking about special memories. This was the place where she stopped seeing me as a stranger, and I became a friend.

"Blanche, what I'm looking for from you is some of history about the Katy community. I wanted to go back in time and capture some of what the city was like."

"Well I am eighty-eight years old. My husband was the first fire chief here in Katy; he got the ambulance here in town for the city. My father was a rice farmer. First of all, my brother played six-man football. His name is Melvin Jordan."

"Oh my, Blanche, I didn't realize the connection here. I met your brother Melvin at Richard's wake. He is Charlie Shafer's father-in-law!"

"Yes that's right! Melvin was the quarterback on that

team. My son was on the first eleven-man team that won State in 1959. My nephews Richard and Bill Jordan were on that team as well. Those boys lived at my house, and what made that team so wonderful was that they were so close. They were like a knitted family. I took care of Farriel Culpepper. His folks were in Brookshire, and they had left. I believe that they moved up in East Texas somewhere. So Cully didn't have a place to stay, and he moved in with us.

"They were all so close. The boys, who lived in Addicks, after practice, would all come over to my house until their parents could come and get them. Of course, they were hungry when they got here. They would bring their old, dirty uniforms, so our washing machine was always on the run. Usually about six or eight extras would hang out here. Of course, I would call Coach Brown and his wife to let them know that the boys were all here, so I would invite them to come out and join us as well.

"We would have all the coaches over: Gordon, Joe, and Fred would come by and join the boys for dinner."

"What made this team so close," I asked?

"The coaches were here as much as the kids were. I believe that when you do things together outside of the game of football, that the kids just seemed to like each other better. They became good friends.

"When Cully would get beside himself and get a big head after seeing his face in the paper, my son would tell the line not to block for him in practice. Well, Cully would come back home and say, 'Ma, they just did me in today.' I would say, 'What happened, Cully?' Of course, I knew what had happened. Well, nobody thought that I was that important. Then he wouldn't speak to Dwayne when he came home. Of course, that never stopped him from eating, though.

"He [Cully] could eat four or five eggs and a half a

gallon of milk almost. He was a good kid, and it was pleasure to have him around. He and my son were always tied at the hip.

"This place was like a hotel here on Friday afternoons; most of the boys would meet here and get themselves ready before they caught the bus and set off for the ball game. We were living over on Franz Road at the time. I would come in, and there would be boys all over the place. Off the field was the most important part of that team...keeping them together. If they got upset at one another, they got over it pretty quick.

"Dwayne, not because he was my son, happened to be a good leader. He would demand from his teammates 'a little more.' Believe it or not, the boys really listened to him, no matter what the situation was. All the boys loved to be around us. Gordon, my husband, and I just loved kids. We raised a lot of kids in this town while we were here. Most of them didn't belong to us! Kids had a chance to talk with us about anything. Sometimes, kids just need to talk to someone, and it makes them feel better about things.

"If things were not going like they wanted it to - on or off the field - they would come and talk to Dwayne about it. They would talk to the coaches. Those coaches were like fathers to those kids. The coaches were always there for everything that involved the boys, whether it was about football or not. The kids really loved Gordon Brown because he was a part of not only football, but he was a part of their lives. He did a lot of molding of their character.

"His first wife Jennie was like a stepmother to the kids. She loved those kids, too. She would come by and bring cookies that she had made for the boys. Those boys are still close today."

"It is funny that you said that, Blanche. I had a chance

to see Coach Brown with a small group of the players together over at Rhodes stadium for a photo shoot once. You could still see the connection that they had with him. It was like they were still kids. Even Coach Brown was in a place where you could tell that he was very comfortable."

"Just like today, the parents back then were really involved with the team; of course we were a lot smaller back then. Everybody in town was sort of connected in some way. They were either kin, or they were real close friends. So, they were interested in every kid that was on that team. The closeness of the whole community was the great thing about Katy back then."

"What made the community so close at that time, Blanche?"

"Well, the football team made it that way. Everybody became a part of that football team. Mr. Dube, who had a store in town, would donate anything that was needed if you had a reception or anything. The merchants would say, 'What do you need?' and be happy to give it to support the team back then. So, everyone would rally around the team to help make it better. People back then believed in the spirit of the community. They created that spirit by being a part of it.

"Pat Adams, who was the Chief of Police at that time, was sort of a part of everything too. He saw that the kids got home at the right time. Gene Cullen was the Assistant Chief; there were only two of them in Katy at that time. They both looked after the kids. The whole town looked after the kids. If someone needed a sports coat, or something, we made sure that they found one somewhere.

"One thing that I notice about today is that people don't make the time to put into the kids like we did back then. Even my kids, they don't slow down to take the time to just relax. Everybody is always on the go. We took the time to relax back then. I think that is what helped us to live longer.

"Well, by the time that Katy made it to the playoffs, there was nobody left in the town. Everybody was so involved in the program that the town was left empty! My husband was in charge of getting buses for everyone to drive up to that State game. So, we got about four buses to help carry the town to that game.

"We didn't buy a lot of stuff back then. Most of the stuff we made ourselves. Everybody seemed to work together. It was something that, to this day, I will never forget - the closeness of this community. As we got larger, I watched a lot of that closeness disappear. Today, you hardly know your next-door neighbors. People stopped waving to each other anymore."

I knew what Blanche was saying had a lot of merit to it. Times had brought about some real changes in society. It sounded like she had stumbled across a few things that had helped to make Katy High School football so great, although I knew that some of the elements were still around. They had just taken on different names and sizes, like the Katy High School Football Booster Club. There are still parents who go out of their way to help support all the school's programs. However, today, they carry the power and weight of a political machine.

"It was just that back then, things were a little simpler in life. We didn't have a lot of money to buy things, so we just made what we could. We made our on soap back then. Another thing was that we were not in such a big hurry back then. Today's generation always seems to be in such a hurry. They don't take the time to enjoy life."

Right on cue, Blanche's grandson walked in the door. He sat down for about three minutes and joined the conversation. Suddenly, his cellular phone rang, and in less than thirty seconds, he was back out the door. Blanche looked at me and smiled. "You see what I mean; we didn't have those cell phones back then. As a matter of fact we made the box for our phone in the house. The phone lines went into everybody's home back then. You knew it was for you according to the number of rings. Many times, everybody in town would be listening to your conversation.

"I remember one time, when Dwayne was first born, that he had a cold and had trouble breathing. So, I called the operator to find the doctor. Well, someone else interrupted the call and said, 'Put a tent over him and get some boiling water and put turpentine in it.' We didn't have Mentholatum back then. But she had forgotten that she was listening on the line and just yelled out the instructions to help get Dwayne better.

Elisabeth Clyett was the operator back then, and you could call her if there was a fire out in the country, and she would call everyone. If somebody died, you would call her, and she would say, 'I will take care it.' She would call all your relatives and pass the news along. She absolutely kept in contact with everybody. That was the closeness of the community back then."

"Blanche, I have uncovered the fact that church was a big part of things back then."

"It was. I believe that Gordon Brown had a lot to do with that because he believed in the boys going to church. Whether they did or not, he did not preach it, he just suggested that they be in church. Gordon was really good, not only in football, but in making the boys into good people. He really was concerned about that. You never saw any of those football boys go any place that they were not dressed and clean. Times were hard back then, and people had to make sacrifices for some of the little things."

"Blanche, what was the political climate like at that time?"

"Well, this was around the time that the Humble Refinery plant came around. Katy was not really ready to include the Humble group in at the time. In those days, it took time to bring in new ideas, no matter what they were. Most of the people from the refinery started to go to our churches and eventually became a part of our community and helped us to grow. They just had to grow on us, I guess.

"Another thing that happened when the boys were growing up - Gordon, my husband, would let Dwayne have the pickup, and he would go around town and pick up the other boys on the team and bring them back here. Now, the Newman boys, they would get into a fight with each other every day. So, one of the kids would come and say, 'The Newmans are at it again.' Gordon would say, 'Let them fight through it.' Dwayne was not old enough to have a license, but he would gather all the boys together and bring them by to play football in the yard. Then, he would take them all home. Those kids played together off the field.

"You know that Gordon Brown did not have a lot to pick from back then. But somehow, he made a team out of what he had. Somehow he managed to get the very best out of the boys, and they played hard for him too. The boys didn't really expect a lot back then. They loved playing football, and they enjoyed being with one another. After football, they were always together. They were a family. Our family here was the first to get a school together for a dance. You really didn't have things like that back then. We had to sign our life away just to put together the first dance for the boys and girls at the time.

"I am so glad to see that Katy is successful today with their football team. And I thank you for writing this book because the kids should never forget where they have come from…the way the world was back then."

Walking into a person's life as a stranger and leaving as a friend is a special part of researching for this book. Each interview somehow helped me to unravel the big mystery that has created Katy's football program. Like all of the interviews before this one, again I was given a path to take and person to see next. I knew that I was about to knock at the door of Mr. Melvin Jordon.

Continuing the Tiger Connection
The Melvin Jordon Story

Finding Melvin Jordan was not a difficult task for me, after all I had been given his number in one of my first interviews by his son-in-law, Charlie Shafer. I didn't know at the time just how important Melvin was to the Katy Tiger connection. It appeared that early Katy was all about family and friends. No doubt, this helped to keep the community very close.

Upon hearing that Melvin was the brother of Blanche, I knew that I had to get his words on early Katy. I remembered the first time that we met that I felt that his thoughts would be worth a truckload of memories. Melvin is a young man trapped in an older man's body. His energy seems to brighten the day of anybody around him. I first perceived this when I met him at Richard Fussell's wake.

After I placed a call to Melvin after the Fussell interview, he and I decided to meet at the local town breakfast place named Snappy's. I remembered that a barber at the Olde Town Barber Shop named Scott told me about Snappy's when I first began to research the book. "Hey, if you want to find out about the history of Katy, just go up and ask somebody over at Snappy's." Life has a way of running full circle at times. Our meeting was scheduled around 8:30 on Friday morning.

I walked up to the waitress behind the register and told her that I was meeting Melvin Jordon. She pointed over into the corner. There he was, sitting and already starting his first cup of coffee. "Mr. Jordon, thank you for meeting with me."

"Oh, call me Melvin," he said. Melvin's distinctive look made it obvious that, at one time, he had been a very important part of the community. You could just tell by the way he carried himself that he was confident and self-assured about his place in life. Time was an ally to him, and it was written in his smile. At the table, I did not hesitate to activate my memory box. I knew from the beginning that I didn't want to miss one word that came out of his mouth.

"Mr. Jordon, were you on the first Katy tiger football team?"

"No, I was not on the first team. I was on the 1941 six-man team. Coach Reader was the first coach, but he only lasted a couple of years. Then - most people don't know this - but we had a coach that was a Baptist preacher. His name was Blackmon. His brother was the superintendent at the time. We here pretty shabby back then. There was some outside help working with us, as well. The next year after that, we had a guy by the name of Edward Lee Bailey as the Coach in 1944."

"Do you remember much about Coach Reader?"

"I remember Ned; he was a big husky fellow. The football field was right over where the old elementary school is today."

"I hear that it was in pretty bad shape."

Smiling back at me, he said, "Well, in the summer we used it as the rodeo grounds. It was used for goat roping and calf roping. In the football season, we just had a smooth wire around it. Then, people with cars would drive right up to the wire border and sit out on the hoods of their cars and watch the game. They were literally parked about eight feet off the sideline. There was a small section of stands for the band.

"Today, you have all the environmental laws in place, but again, back then, times were different. My father Hank

Jordon was a school board member. A little story about my father: Football was not a big-time sport like it is today, back in my time. Most people didn't even know about it back then, including my father. Well, I asked my father if I could play, and he said no. Somehow, I managed to talk him into at least letting me practice with the team. One afternoon, he came to a game, and my coach put me in the game. My dad was hooked on football from that very moment on. He never missed a game after that.

"My second year on the team - we needed some suits. The school didn't have any money. Before then, we played in these old yellow uniforms that felt like cardboard. Some dads got together and decided to buy eight new red suits. It was my dad, Mr. Charlie Carter, and Mr. Morrison who went down and started the red suit tradition"

"How many fans did you have back in those early years, Mr. Jordon?"

"Oh, it was hard to say. I remember all the cars lined up completely around the football field. I'm thinking that it was a little around fifty to a hundred. Like I said, many folks simply didn't know about the game back then.

"Here's something, Dexter, that I bet you didn't know. Back then, I had a couple of older brothers who played basketball, and they played on dirt courts right there by the old school. This was before the school got a gym."

"You mean, they actually played games on the dirt courts?"

"Oh yeah, Addicks, Waller, and Cypress. It was just a dirt court. They didn't play much baseball back then. When football was introduced, it grew rapidly. My last year at Katy, we were undefeated. We played Danberry down there in the mud and rain. We had a heck of a crowd.

"I could not really tell you how many people were

there. When you are seventeen or eighteen years old, you really do not pay much attention to how many people are following you."

"Mr. Jordon, what position did you play?" "Well,   I would have been what you called a quarterback back then. We lined up three on the ball. Then we would have the two in the backfield, then me in the middle. I was the smallest on the team, but I was pretty quick in those days. We didn't have really big people back then. Earnest Bishop weighed about a hundred and ninety; he was our biggest player on the team. We thought that he was a bull in those days.

"Most of the big guys back in my day were pretty slow. We used to laugh and say that they were so big that they would run like a dry creek. It meant that they could not get around, which was to my advantage. Again, football was a new sport, but we all could tell that it was going to catch on.

"I had a couple of brothers that were quiet a few years older than me, Chester and Leonard. My wife Bertye and I married right out of high school The next to play football at Katy was Bill Jordan, and then there was my nephew Dwayne Fussell. Charlie, who was on that 1959 team, married my daughter.

"Next to come along, was my son Steve who was the quarterback on the 1961 or 1962 team, I believe. Then, we followed the grandkids through Katy.

"When I was in high school, I guess that there were about two hundred and fifty kids in the district."

"That is amazing. Today, Katy has over 50,000 kids in Katy ISD."

Where Bertye and I live right now used to be an old dirt road, and maybe ten cars a day would go by. You didn't even have to look up back then, and you could just listen and tell whose vehicle was passing by. Today, you can barely get out of my driveway, so many cars go flying by."

"Did you farm out here?"

"Oh yes, I farmed rice out here for fifty-six years and quit about five years ago. I am still running cattle; that's about all I do now - the cattle business. It's been a good life around here, hard struggles up and down, yet we always came out stronger for some reason. This is a very special community."

Smiling to myself, I thought I was becoming well aware of that phrase. I asked, "What about the community back then?"

"Back in 1959, when the first State football team was going, me and my wife had a store right over there on 2nd Street." He pointed almost directly across the streets from the Snappy's restaurant. "She ran the department store; I didn't. It was right over there, across from the hardware store; it was called Ber Mel's. Times were different back time; if you came into the store, and one the girls was busy, you just grabbed what you needed, held it up, and said, 'Hey, just put this on my account.' We didn't know what cash was around that time. It was that way all over in this little area of town.

"Everybody knew what everybody was doing; if anybody had troubles, somebody was there. We opened that store back in 1956. We had the old crank phone systems back then with the old party lines.

"When the phone rang, everybody picked it up. One funny little story that I will always remember when we had our first child, I was in Houston, and I called back home to my dad. I said, 'Dad, we got a boy.' Somebody on the party line said, 'Yippee!' That's just the way it was back in Katy early years.

"That was the kind of community that Katy has

always been. The longer that you stayed on the phone, the more people eventually hung up the phone. They would get their ear full and hang up the line. The community back in the '50s and '60s has always been a good community. Most people back then had some kind of small business. The gas plant came in around '40 or '41.

"I just feel blessed for the opportunity to have lived in that period. If you were out in your yard, and people would be driving down the road, they would stop by, just see what you were doing.

"Back to our store, like I said, the older people like we are now would come in and just leave you their list, and we would fill it. We knew them so well, we could do their shopping for them. My wife, on graduation, would go over to Jack Rhodes' office and say, 'I need all the seniors' names and what colors they like, and what they prefer.' He would get it from them for us. Later, people would come in and say, 'I got an invitation to the graduation for so-and-so. I don't really know what they want.' We would already have a list of what the kids wanted and filled it for them, and they would be out the door.

"In most cases we would have the gifts wrapped and already waiting in the window. That's kind of community we had. Back in my early days, there were only about three little grocery stores around. They were very small, and then you had a lumberyard which took care of the hardware needs. This was back in the '40s and '50s.

"It's hard to believe how this little town has grown today. Most people would never imagine what humble beginning that Katy came from by looking at it today.

"Most of the subdivisions that you see today around here were old farms. Back in the '60s and '70s, we were farming over 70,000 acres of rice in this area. In the late '70s, many farmers got into soybeans. Today, I bet there is probably less than 5,000 acres being farmed. This would include up around Waller County.

"Back in my day, most of the boys would do chores before they went off to school. We would milk about three or four cows every morning, and we did not think anything of it. Those were just the times that we lived in. Today, kids walk to the refrigerator and pour a big glass of milk. They do it without thinking that there was a time, not long ago, when this simple act was not available to them.

"I remember being about eight years old before we got our first refrigerator. That was like a special thing back then. We would gather around the box and just watch it keep cold."

"Do you remember anything about the television era?"

"Oh yeah! It was in the early forties - my dad was one of the first ones to get a set out in our area. So, our house became a gathering place for the nights that the Melton Berl show was on television. My dad Hank would love to watch baseball. The deal there was that Dad would turn the volume down on the television set and turn it up on the radio. The announcers in radio were much better than the television broadcast in those days. Of course, there was only the one television channel for a while here.

"Today, times have changed around us. I think that I have somewhere around forty-five relatives, including in-laws around me. Though times have changed, I think what bothers me the most is that there was something special about those times. In a way, though we didn't have a lot, we had it all."

"I understand what you are saying, Mr. Jordon. Back then, the simple fact that we had more respect for our elders helped to create a different social environment for us."

"Yes, yes, the simple words 'Yes Ma'am' or 'No Ma'am,' 'Yes Sir' or 'No Sir' have been lost in the progress of our social development. What really bothers me is the fact that we are losing our morals, and it doesn't seem to bother anyone. Back in my day, you did things with your kids, which helped to protect them from the wild ways of the world.

"We would hunt, fish or swim. They were simple things, but they were things that created time together. Kids could ask us questions about life and open up and talk to us about things concerning them.

"I believe, Dexter, something as simple as people having the chance to sit down at the table together at night and eat was the best form of healing that this country had back in my day. We could get information out of our children - what their fears were. We knew what their concerns were back then. It allowed us to simply come together as one. We take that for granted these days. Everybody had a chance to put their little input into the conversation and feel like they had been heard.

"Kids back in the day were not so rebellious to the fact that they could not do certain things. Those things were discussed. They agreed not to do them, and it was with honor and respect that they would put their feet under the dinner table. They knew how everybody felt. Today little words like 'Please' have slowly faded away from our vocabulary. When we lose the little words, we ultimately lose the core of respect.

"In my time, when we shook hands for a deal, we didn't need contracts or piles of paperwork, we knew we had a deal because of the handshake. You might not even like the fellow, but if you shook hands with him, that was it. It was sealed. This was one of the many things that make this community so special today. Embedded in its heritage lies those old school principals that people keep building on today."

I watched as the waitress placed our ticket on the table. Before I heard the noise of the little tray hitting the table, Mr. Jordan had already claimed the check. "I got this," he said. While we were at the table, a number of his friends came over spoke to him to say hello.

I could tell that he was still a major figure in the Katy community. I felt that sadness coming over me again. It was something that was beginning to become the "norm" with me after finishing up my interviews for *KatyNation*. It is hard to explain, but I have learned that when people give their time to tell you about their lives, there becomes this bond which lets you know that, in some kind of cosmic way, we have become a small part of their past.

I felt even more grateful that I was continuing to uncover the elements that made Katy's football program so grand. This program was not just some super-sized subdivision that sprang up over the weekend. It was the byproduct created from the lives of countless people like Melvin Jordon and his sister Blanche whose hard work and humble spirits were deeply saturated into the heart of Katy.

I wondered if the students who suit up and dominate the gridiron today truly understand the remarkable foundation that lies underneath the football fields that they occupy.

The one thing that I did know for sure that was with each person with whom I talked about Katy's football community, I was being fed a new dose of passion and excitement about this program. If I could find a way to bottle it, I would be able to do something very special to help mankind. For right now, until I can learn to bottle it, I will simply have to "Book It."

What's up, Doc?
The Bing Doctors

You will find him walking the sidelines of many of Katy High School football games. Not just for the Tigers, but also for any Katy ISD school, you can find Dr. Mark Bing pacing the sidelines, as if he were a collegiate football coach, looking like he could be the stunt double for the actor Richard Dryfuss, Dr. Bing watches the success of the Tigers' program just like his father did before him.

A friend of mine Margaret King gave me a number for Dr. Bing earlier in my research of *KatyNation*. It was not until towards the end of the book did I get a chance to catch up with him by scheduling a luncheon one Wednesday afternoon. It seemed the more information that I researched Katy's football history, the more I found myself gaining weight. Dr. Bing invited me to the a little barbecue spot that I had visited before. This is what I learned about his family's Tiger connection.

"My grandfather R.H. worked out on a dairy in the 1920's in Monaville, between Brookshire and Hempstead. Then he moved to East Texas to Oakwood, same place that Roosevelt Alexander is from. By the way, Roosevelt is too shy of a man to tell you what he really meant to this community. He is a great man, truly a great man.

"Surprisingly, Oakwood was a popular place because it had three cotton gins. There were a lot of people who came out of the small little town. Basically, this little-nothing town produced a number of very special people. My dad and his brother went to medical school. My dad was working back in Oakwood for a drug representative. Katy was looking for a doctor."

"Now, when you say a community is 'looking for a doctor,' back in that day, did you have to be selected?"

"No, you just go there and slowly settle in.

"Being the community doctor, he was asked to be on the sidelines for the football games. I'm not really sure how it all happened. I just remember from 1953 or 1954, Dad being a part of the football program."

"Doc, what was your father's biggest challenge back in his day?"

Laughing out loud, he replied, "No MRI machine for starters! Yes, draw that water off your knee. Back then, they had an x-ray machine in the back of the office. The kids would come over after the game, and that was basically all they could offer them back in the day.

"There was a drugstore that was a very central place in the community back in 1959. It was located on 2nd Street in Katy. My dad's office was located right next to it. Most of the kids would get off the school bus there and have their parents pick them up from right there. So, it really was sort of a central place.

"The black and white picture of the '59 team was taken by an Ed Tillerson. Ed was sort of a local photographer, always hanging out at the Katy games. The day after the game, he would have pictures at the drugstore for kids to buy. Now, if you worked at the drugstore, you were considered the coolest kid in school. The guys who did that are still around. Billy Haskett, who is the announcer today at the Katy game, was one of those kids back then.

I remember the kids working behind the soda fountain saying how great it was that we had a championship team. Even though we did not do too much after the '59 season, people had a habit of taking championships for granted. I remember that because it was pretty much the end of the road for the championship years for the Katy Tigers

"We would win in '62 and '63; we managed to reach district or bi-district, even make it to regionals. The Tigers did not see another championship for almost forty years. The thing is that it is easy to take winning for granted. After the early '60s, there was a series of really bad years for the program.

"Things have changed when it comes to head injuries for kids today. We keep them out longer than we did back then. The game today is less dangerous than it was in the early years. You can't do crack back blocks.

"You are not supposed to dive in with your head. So even though the equipment was inferior in the beginning, today, the better equipment and more restrictive rules help to create a safer game.

"Back to the early '80s - it was very bleak in those years. From what I could see, Coach Johnston believed that the big plays were made on the small side of the field. In those years, I found the play calling very simple. It was 'Cantrall right, Cantrall left.' The passing game was not really good; there was no kicking game. There was no kid that could kick a field goal further than twenty yards.

"Though all of that, there was a change in strategy. Mike had a game plan, and he was not going to veer far from the blueprints of his plan. Most of us close to the inside of the program began to see Mike's vision; however, in his early tenure, many in the community were not buying into it at all.

"The reality is that small-town Katy was always grumpy with their coaches if they were not winning. Never mind that in the early years, they did not send their kids to summer training. It was always the coach's fault."

"So, the community in the early years simply demanded excellence without the effort."

"Right, it wasn't until they learned to demand more out of their kids did things start to change. A great example of this was Bubba Fife. This man did more to get scholarships for the kids than anyone one in the history of the Katy coaches. But because he did not win at Katy, he ended up at Taylor High School. This was ridiculous; but did they get their kids to go work out in the summer?"

"So, it is easy to make the argument that some of the losing years of early Katy were attributed to the lack of involvement of parents in the community?"

"Yes, that is a fair assessment, if you are not going to get your kids to work in the off season, or get them into the gym and prepare themselves for the future, this is true. This is one of the things that Mike brought to the community of Katy, the need to prepare year 'round for a successful program.

"Kids started to get into an environment where they began to get committed; they started studying and working out in the off season. That's when things started to change; it was no big mystery. It was hard work, commemorated with an honest desire to do what it took to change the outcome of a losing program.

"You see, there are a couple of things that I think were the key to how all this happened. Not being a coach, but just giving you my perspective - one is the summer participation. You have to do that. The way that this is administered has changed. It used to be that coaches could not have any involvement in the summer programs.

"So, many kids had to go outside the school in order to get the continued work needed to continue their athletic growth. Secondly, the community has to realize that football is an important part of its existence. You have to have kids that will play on the team without respect to individual acknowledgment. Believe me, that is a tough thing to do."

"Yes I know what you mean. There is much more to that kind of sacrifice than meets the eye."

"Because the program focuses on the team concept rather than the individual, kids who don't play as a team are basically eliminated. How that happens, I'm not sure; it is evident that those kinds of players don't seem to stay around very long. The fact that the junior high programs feed the system helps kept the flow of that kind of team concept into the next level.

"From a medical perspective, to me there was another gradual thing that happened which I think was very important, learning to have a better understanding of the mechanics of the human body. You remember the time where you were told not to drink too much water and you were forced to take handfuls of salt pills to play football? Well, we have come a long way from that.

"Today's coaches, because of the different clinics that they attend, which they didn't have years back - well, now they understand how to condition young athletes so that they peak and get stronger toward the end of the season. That is a huge difference. If your coaching program is not searching for ways to separate their team from the pack, then they are literally cheating their own program.

"Many high school teams out there train their kids to peak at the end of district, whereas here, these kids are trained to peak at the end of the playoff year.

"Big difference, this is something that slides under the radar with many high school programs. Another thing, I bet that you don't remember eating during a game, do you? Well, we believe that light fruit...bananas, grapes, power bars...help to create better athletes towards the end of the game. So, we give them complex carbohydrates to help get them the energy that they need to finish stronger.

"The last thing is what did you do on Monday after you have played on Friday night? You got back out on the field and worked your butt off, right? Here, these kids get a day to recover, so [the coaches] put them into the pool. The kids get to work the lactic acids out, and they are 'good to go' on Tuesday."

"I am curious, Doc, does Katy have this knowledge, and others don't?"

"I think that Katy coaches search out all opportunities to improve themselves with clinics, seminars and classes."

"So, Doc. You are ultimately saying that the coaches here simply work harder to educate themselves in an effort to get a better understanding so that they can give their program a better chance at success."

"That's it in a nut shell."

"I guess that this is the kind of commitment that the outside world never considers when viewing the success of this football program. But this is something that is accessible to all high school programs right?"

"Yes, it is! The coaches here, just like the players, work just as hard in the off season to prepare themselves for the next year."

"Doc, it sounds like you have seen a lot in your years at Katy. I just have to ask you about your perspective of the year that the kids were taken off the bus and disqualified."

"Oh, 'the Grinch that stole Christmas.' Listen, I'm still pretty bitter about that story. I still have my non-refundable tickets hanging on my walls. It really made me sad. I was so mad about that. I had to go to Odessa to give a talk on medicine. Damn, if they didn't have the ball from that game in the airport.

"People still talk about that episode in Katy's history;

however, to this day, many people don't realize that there was more than one infraction to that story. This offers me a little different perspective, even though it still hurt the same. Here's what many people didn't know. That year, Katy was very powerful. It was a great football team. B.C. was there at middle linebacker, just an incredible athlete. We thought that he was going to "play on Sundays."

"Well, there was another kid who got to play who was ineligible academically earlier in the year. Katy was already on probation for an episode which included feeding the team at a place called Joe's Crab Shack. Kids were charged five bucks, and the Booster Club was supposed to pick up the rest of the tab. Well, that never happened.

"So the team would have to forfeit all the games up to that point, meaning that they would have to have won the rest of their games to win district. They were already in the 'appealing' status of that ruling, when the situation with the ineligible kid came along."

"So, in reality, it was a combination of the two things that cause the UIL ruling to take place."

"Yes, I think that it was an unfair assessment. But from the UIL perspective, 'You're on probation, and you broke the rules.' That was it.

"As for the last kid that was found ineligible, he received great advice. He wrote a letter to the community. It was a well-constructed letter, carefully crafted. I found that it was impossible that he wrote the letter himself because of the fact that the course [in which] he was found ineligible was an English course. However, the spirit of the letter came across very well."

Doc and I finished our lunch that afternoon. He had helped to add to my understanding about the heart and soul that lives with in the Katy community.

Interview after interview left me carrying a little part of this community back with me. The one thing that came to the forefront with each person with whom I talked was his or her unquestioned passion for the Katy football program. Whether their involvement was twenty years ago or on the field today, these characters remain loyal to the Katy Tiger cause.

A Kodak Moment
Nick Georgandis Story

You can find them running up and down the sidelines of many high school games. Like giant bees, they swamp back and forth, trying to get into that special spot to capture the perfect shot. If they were in Hollywood, they would be called paparazzi. Here in Texas, they are just hard-working folks whose love for the game of football has them taking pictures of every down of every game.

They are men and women who carry, sometimes, two or three cameras in order to get the shot that every sports fans would love to see, the shot that will find its life in the eyes of a reader. Week after week, this procedure recurs. Then, the cycle starts all over again at the next week's game. Most people take for granted the pictures that confront them in the sports section of their local paper each day. They never question what the person taking the pictures had to go through to capture that shot. Photographers are like artists. Each shot carries the love of their craft. Nick Georgandis is one of those who can be found roaming the sidelines at every Katy High School football game. Most people would say that he is just doing his job, which happens to be that of the sports editor of the *Katy Times* newspaper.

Nick is not the kind who sits behind a desk all day and bosses interns around, like you see in the movies. Nick happens to be a true Tiger fan, even though he has sworn allegiance to all of the Katy ISD programs.

I first told you about him at the beginning of my research. Since then, I have had the opportunity to watch him from a distance, and I can easily see his passion for Katy football. I caught up with Nick one afternoon over at the *Katy*

Times office. He had just been promoted to his new position, and it was nice to see that those at the *Times* also appreciated his hard work.

The *Katy Times* is nestled in the heart of old town Katy. It was there that I had a chance to get an inside look into the day and the life of a newspaper editor.

"Come on in and have a seat." Nick had his busy face on, so I took my recorder out early in order to make every moment count.

"Nick, where did you go to school?"

"I went to Bellaire High School and then to A&M. I was the sports editor of the paper there for about four or five semesters. Then, I took a job in a little town named Paris, Texas. I lasted there about a week and a half before I realized this was not going to be me. All you had to do was drive around for a few minutes, and it was easy to see where your future was going.

"From there, I went over to Rice University and worked in their athletic department as a media guy. As I was moving out of that job, I had two interviews: one in Conroe and one in Katy. Literally, about fifteen minutes before going to Conroe, I got the Katy offer. So, I was the sports editor here from '97 to this past May. I came here in July of 97."

"Oh, so you arrived the year before Katy got pulled off the bus?"

"Yes, I very well remember pulling up in my Volkswagen Beetle at the Astrodome in '97, thinking that this might be the biggest thing that might ever hit the cover, so I better really enjoy it. Well, they have won two more since then and played for two others. Then in '98…the kids not being able to go…that was a real test of the community."

"Nick, I'm curious about what kept this community together, and how it managed not to fall apart when that happened."

"Well, I think that it has a lot to do with those in the old part of Katy that find themselves in the heart of the community. It's a small part of the city, but the part that has all the heritage and is very steeped in religion. It has that very strong family unit. Not to downplay the suburbs, because I live in one, but you don't see that remarkable bond in the large cities as much as you do in the smaller communities."

"Why is that Nick, why don't you see that? I mean if everybody knew that it took this kind of foundation to be successful, wouldn't you think that everyone one would make that adjustment"?

"Well sure, let's see, I should I say this: I think that it has a lot to do with economics, in that when there are people that are my age and younger having kids, and they have those big-time jobs and that will pay them enough money to buy a house like in Cinco Ranch...they expect things to come quick.

"Let's say that I have a job as an engineer and I make $150,000.00 dollars a year. I can buy myself a great home, a nice car. My kids are in grade school, and I'm getting them everything they need. What happens is people expect that to translate into winning, but it doesn't always. It's not that there is anything wrong with that reality. But, I think that the 'good things that come to those that wait' mentality, accompanied by the understanding that you really, really have to work, does have a great impact. Especially in a game like football where you have to 'get tough in the trenches' kind of thing."

"That is an interesting perspective, Nick. It is one that I did not even consider before."

"You know, there is a lot of camaraderie at other schools. But here in Katy, kids say that they want to be like the winning tradition. I mean, you either buy into tradition or you don't. I mean, if a school thinks that they can just win it for themselves, that's another thing, and it takes a lot of talent to do that. But, if you are trying to win for all those that came before you, then, to me, that says a lot"

"I have to agree with that, Nick. When you look at the teams that have been more successful, they are the programs that are rich in heritage."

"Yes, Katy has played some great teams in the playoffs, teams with so much more athletic ability, it's ridiculous. When they would come to the Astrodome, they would bring 150 people to watch them play in the playoffs. Then you look on the other side, and Katy has over fifteen thousand."

"When did you become aware, Nick, that you had tapped into something very special here in Katy?"

"When I first got here. I didn't really know what was going on. I barely knew any of the players. I mean, I was only twenty-three, for one thing. I was just a little older than most of the kids. At that time, Mayde Creek, one of our other schools, was almost as good that year. They went very far in the playoffs that year as well. They have not been back since. I want to say that they were 10-2 in '97.

"I would say that it wasn't until 1999 that I really start to realize what a super-special program this was. I mean, the seniors from the 1998 team were something else. They came back and told the team to get back to that state game for us. You had a quarterback that never lost a start and a running back that probably put up over 3600 yards in two years. That team had some of their best defenders ever.

"1999 was a really young team. Let's see how they started off. Well, they lost their homecoming. They were beating people but not by a whole lot. They made it up to the State Championship game. For those kids to get all the way back was something pretty special."

"Nick, one of the things that I find so amazing about the Tigers' program is the number of players whose fathers and grandfathers were once a part of the football program."

"Yes, Dex, I know what you mean. We did a big special section for the 25th year of the district. When Taylor started, we went from being Katy to Katy ISD. I went through and got every score from 1980 on. It was incredible to see just how many people [there were] who had older brothers who played. I have covered at least three or four brother combinations since I have been here."

"You look like you really fit in here, Nick."

"Well, from Coach Johnston to Coach Joseph, they have really embraced me here. That is one of the things that have made it so easy to stay around all this time. Many of the players that I see come back have shown their appreciation. Some of the coaches today are guys that I covered back then when I first got here, Coach Landers for one. He was on that 1998 team, and they had a powerful defense. They had a couple of shutouts in the playoffs. He made First Team All-State in 1997."

"Why is it, Nick, that Katy has such an incredible program and not have kids who are going on to play big-time collegiate and pro ball?"

"That is an interesting question. My first year here, they actually had several that went on to play for strong college programs and the one now, Eric Heitman, who went on to play for the Forty Niners. I think the coaches, along with the tradition and the discipline, can get more out of an average kid than most coaches can. The coaches drill the kids that, 'This is your role, and if you do your role right, we are going to win, no matter who we are playing.'

"Even when Katy does have great athletes, they are

usually undersized. I really don't know why that is. Another thing that I feel is that most collegiate recruiters are mostly blind to what a good football player is as opposed to what is a good athlete."

"Yes, I know, they are more into 'size and size and more size.'"

"For instance, Will Thompson. This kid is a great athlete. He's having a great year up at Blinn Junior College, and there is no reason for him being looked over, none whatsoever. He can play multi positions. I am praying that A&M gets him. I can't believe that Texas Tech or someone didn't take a chance on him. He went to the All Star game in December and simply abused the opposing team.

"I got to see him every single game that he played from his sophomore year on. I mean, if you had a picture of a Katy Tiger in the dictionary, Will would be right there. I saw his interception against Chase Daniels, who is now the starting quarterback at Missouri.

"I mean, every single game, you felt like he was going to do something to change the completion of the game. They brought Will up on special teams; then, he started making plays until he got into the starting line up. He came in his first game on varsity, I think that he recovered a punt and blocked a punt, too.

"I have to say that going to a Katy game is like going to a big party for me. All my friends are there. I go take my pictures, but it's the kind of job that you want to have, one that you truly enjoy what you are doing."

"Nick, when you see this program up close and personal each week, tell me what goes through your mind?"

"Well, I am always amazed how, 'on paper,' people write this program off. Yet, they always find a way to work their way into the playoffs. Even when they get knocked off, it's by somebody like Vince Young over at Madison.

"My case in point: in a couple of weeks Katy will play Cinco Ranch. Both teams are undefeated right now. Cinco is playing extremely well. They have a great offensive line, a good strong quarterback this year. But as sure as we are sitting here, it will be Katy's tradition that will be the equalizing factor in that ball game. I have seen it over and over.

"Katy will come out and toss that player into the air; they will have their band playing and their drill team and cheerleaders hopping around all over the place. The whole crowd knows exactly what the team is going to do. Let's say if Katy scores first on their opponents, Katy fans then feel that strong tradition. There is no way around it; for a lot of [opposing] teams, the game is over. They are not going to come back.

"It is truly is a wonderful thing."

I could tell that Nick was excited about what he was saying, I could see it in his eyes.

"A couple of years ago there was almost the same situation with Katy and Cinco that happened. They both started the season out 8-0, and it was a daytime game, and Rhodes Stadium was completely sold out. Cinco was shattering all their own offensive records that they had, and they had the ball first. On the first play, one of Katy's big linebackers Paul Thornton came around and popped Cinco's quarterback from behind, and that game was over. They ended up losing 38-7. It was never close. Cinco ended up losing the next game after that as well."

"I did not realize Cinco even had that kind of competitive program. Their coach was a product from Katy's wasn't he?"

"Yes, Coach Clayton. He really is one of my better

friends in this district. He got off to a rough start early on, but after he settled in, Cinco's program really started to grow. He was Katy's offensive coordinator for two stretches, one in the early '90s and then again in the late '90s. I think that he and Coach Joseph were both candidates for Cinco Ranch. Of course, Coach Joseph was still at Katy.

"Well, Clayton was the quarterback's coach at Katy, and let me tell you, they had phenomenal quarterbacks in the late '90s. They had Matt Gore, who was the quarterback in '97-'98, he never lost as a starter, 29-0. Matt quarterbacked the '97 team to the title. In '98, they went 15-0 on the field, even though they had to forfeit some of those games.

"The guy that came after him was Jerry Kaspar; he went 14-2 as a junior and 16-0 as a senior. Clayton taught both of them, as well As Rob Peters in '94. When they went to State, Kaspar went on and had a great career at Tech.

"Taylor beat Katy in 1995, which was the last time that the Tigers have lost to a Katy ISD team. It was on a desperate seventy-yard pass in the last minute. Katy's long-time tradition, embodied into its ever-present, small-time community feel, is what keeps Katy special."

I knew that Nick and I could have gone on talking for hours about Katy football. Nick has a deep voice and sounds a lot like the old-time sportscaster from Houston, Ron Franklin, who is now working with ESPN. I see Nick each week on the sidelines.

After talking to him, I realized that what made him so good at his job was his knowledge of the game and his love for the Katy community. Just how the city of Katy manages to find so many quality people is still a mystery. But, whatever it is helps to keep this community special.

Walking Among Tigers

If it is in man to question the true power of thought, then let me set the record straight. The power of our thoughts is real. In the fall of 2005 at Tulley Stadium, I had my first opportunity to see the Tigers play against Smithson Valley. It was my first outside view of the Katy football program. More importantly, it was the inception of the thought which manifested itself into this book, *KatyNation*.

Watching the Tigers play Memorial High at that same stadium a year later, this time from the Tigers' sidelines, that thought had manifested itself into a second book, *KatyNation2*. (Hey, if Hollywood can create a sequel, why can't I?) One idea that became increasingly clear to me is that our thoughts can become reality. After all, it was only a little over a year ago that the suggestion to write a book on the Katy High School football program came to me.

We all have the ability to pursue our positive thoughts and watch them grow. If you get nothing else from this book, know that you have the power to take your thoughts and change the course of your world.

At first, I wondered where to begin and what direction to take in order to write *KatyNation*. However, the book seemed to write itself when I took a step in the direction of my desire. Every once in a while, we come across a project that carries an apparently built-in instruction manual. This manual helps to guide us as we learn to embrace our goal without fear of failure or disappointments. *KatyNation* came with such a manual, and its directions carried me every step of the way through to its completion. This story, in many ways, was written long before I managed to stumble over it. The characters of its past lay waiting for someone to come along and acknowledge their presence,

I am honored because that first someone was found in me. The names and faces that presented themselves are people who have found ways to be true in mind, body, and spirit. Whether you agree with their thoughts or not, I assure you that as I looked into their eyes and hearts and heard them speak, I saw only the love and passion for the football program of which they were once a great part.

Looking at the overall picture of this special football community, it is easy to see the possibilities of an entire volume of information. My challenge to the next generation of writers is to make it so! Don't be afraid to gather your thoughts and watch them grow into the next best seller about this special community.

To think that life has it own wonderful way of tapping us on the shoulder and saying, "Stop, look around. Now, see just what you have left behind for others to grow from," has always been a very special affirmation for me. It confirms that we all affect the lives of others, whether we like it or not. All of us, those acknowledged here have something very special to offer this world.

Learning what that affirmation is sometimes occurs many years into our journeys. When life calls our names, and we turn around, what is it that we will see?

The people in this community make no bones about cherishing the football program that was created in 1939, a time when the game was still in its infancy. In little towns across America, football was still sprouting like vigorous weeds in the front and back yards of every city, large and small.

Writing *KatyNation* confronted me with a number of legitimate questions which I'm sure many in the outside world were also asking. It is a common characteristic of humanity to want to find out what others have that they do not. Thus, asking the question, "What does the Katy football program have that the rest of the world doesn't?" is not abnormal.

Katy's program spans well over sixty-seven years. For over half of that time, the Tigers have had a "five hundred" or better season and have racked up more than thirty-five years of winning seasons. Considering that most schools can boast of barely five to ten years of winning seasons, it's no wonder that the Katy Tigers are the envy of the high school world.

The big question is whether or not there can be one common denominator that determines the success of this program. That is the key question that I wanted to uncover and the key answer that I sought. When I present my findings to you, I do so with a very humble spirit and a true conviction for my findings. Many of you, I'm sure, were able to uncover the countless clues that I planted along the way.

There will be many who will not understand. That's quite all right. For the countless communities across America that are looking for ways to change the complexion of their football programs into the kind that Katy High School enjoys, Katy football is the perfect template. Those groups who truly wish to change their program will be listening a little more intently than most. To you still searching, this is what I have found.

First of all, we must never underestimate the power of athletics in our American society. Its growth has managed to bring together once-divided races of humanity and present mankind with an opportunity to challenge our differences on courts and fields throughout the land. "Just a foolish game," you say? I think not. Athletics, in my opinion, has done more to battle the injustices of America's racism than any other antidote throughout history.

The fact that so many interracial teams take the fields and courts today without many of us looking at the colors of skin is a testament to our growth as a nation. For that reason, I say "Thank you" for the games that are played in every high school stadium across our nation.

Secondly, it is important for us to remember the competitive spirit of nearly all living creatures. Mankind's competitive spirit encourages physical and mental contests. In the United States at the high school level, physical competition is one of the purest forms of athletics present in our society today because it is not tainted by the almighty dollar which pollutes the professional arena. High school sports still have an innocence that continues to attract the masses.

We who continue to support high school athletics enjoy the spirit of being young and competitive. We watch the students demonstrate talents, while we cheer in support as if there is no tomorrow.

Once the students and teams earn success, the more they are challenged to maintain it. How any team manages to maintain success in the question that everyone wants answered. This is the question asked by every opponent that has ever faced the roar of the Katy Tigers from KatyNation.

If I were to say that it takes great sacrifices to be as successful as the Katy Tigers, I would not scratch the surface of what is required. One might consider that every high school football program makes sacrifices each and every season, so why are they not having the same successful results as the Katy Tigers?

I knew that you might ask that question, so here is my answer. Yes, it is true that programs all across the country are also making great sacrifices. For the Tigers, sacrifice is not the bottom line. It is merely one of many ingredients listed in the cookbook of their success.

Throughout *KatyNation*, I have included information that I believe will clarify what makes Katy's football program special. In most cases, you have heard these elements directly from "the horse's mouth," as they say in my old neighborhood. The basic principals of commitment, preparation, consistency, selflessness, dedication, discipline, confidence, courage, good character, respect, leadership, guidance, and motivation are all elements that most programs strive to accomplish. However, the Katy Tigers' program already has these elements embedded in the fabric of its foundation.

Fortunately, many other programs also have these elements in their foundations. Therefore, allow me to share with you the one quality which helps the Katy Tigers to stand above the others. Here it is: the one key that countless Katy opponents all over Texas are waiting to discover.

I stumbled across this truism early in the beginning of my research. I assure you that it has taken all of my willpower not to tell you until now. There will be many who will understand exactly what I am saying and who will smile and agree in silence. What the Katy High School football program has that many others don't is something that every program would like, but few have found.

It is with everything good and real inside of me that I

share what I have found. I believe that what this program has achieved that many others have not managed to accomplish is simply because of the strong and consistent Christian beliefs and ethics of many of the participants.

The common denominator that has surfaced throughout my research has been the foundation of Christ. Every cell in my being tells me that this is what separates Katy's program from the rest. This truth lies in the heart of every successful coach who has led these Tigers.

It is found in their faith, dedication, actions, and most of all, their love for Katy's program. I won't debate this; I don't need to defend what I have seen with my own eyes. In a time when most of society removes itself from any acknowledgment of Christ in schools and tiptoes around whether or not it is politically correct to pray in school, this program has managed to find a way to acknowledge His presence. It is an acknowledgment that wants be shouted from the rooftops or seen boastfully parading the streets of Katy's community.

Found in the hearts of young warriors, their coaches, and the families who cheer them is the foundation of faith, courage, conviction, humility and most of all, the love of Christ.

Closing out this journey, I thank those of you who have joined me. For it has been a clear and wonderful year me. The tears that fell from my face as I drove back into Houston from my twenty-year stay in Los Angeles have now been replaced with the joy of having been given the opportunity to share this true story of the history of the Katy High School football program with you.

There are countless uncovered names and faces that lie waiting to be revealed. My wish is that this book will inspire others to give those names a chance to be seen and heard. Writing this book has been a writer's dream; to that I humbly say, "Thank you."

As for that common denominator, believe me when I tell you that it can be found within us all. We simply have to create the thought which takes us beyond the course of action and add works to our faith.

~~The End~~

The Beginning

KatyNation2

Printed in the United States
68815LVS00001BA/1-114

9 780966 544435